So You Wanna Buy A House!

Secrets for Successful House Hunting

by

Corinne T. Luna

Bloomington, IN  Milton Keynes, UK

authorHOUSE™

AuthorHouse™
1663 Liberty Drive, Suite 200
Bloomington, IN 47403
www.authorhouse.com
Phone: 1-800-839-8640

AuthorHouse™ UK Ltd.
500 Avebury Boulevard
Central Milton Keynes, MK9 2BE
www.authorhouse.co.uk
Phone: 08001974150

First published by AuthorHouse 5/12/2006

ISBN: 1-4259-1963-4 (sc)

Printed in the United States of America
Bloomington, Indiana

This book is printed on acid-free paper.

DEDICATION

This book is dedicated to my husband John for his love, constant encouragement, and undying support; to my children Lae Tesia, Amanda, and Marissa who have made me accomplish more than I ever dreamed; to my granddaughter Ahlauna Michele for giving me yet another reason to embrace the day; to my sisters Lorraine and Serena for their love, support and administrative assistance in completing this work.

To the God of the Universe, the God of Abraham and Isaac I pledge my life always, my hands and my feet to be a vessel for your imprint in the land.

TABLE OF CONTENTS

ARE YOU READY?

I decided to write this handbook after working with many nervous buyers during the process of buying a home. No matter how detailed the explanation of what would transpire during the transaction, they would have a frightened look on their faces all the way to the closing table. I believe that buyer anxiety is directly related to trust. Let's face it, buying a home is a major financial investment. Making such an investment for the first time is additionally stressful. To top things off, the total transaction is a marriage of sorts between complete strangers.

Each real estate transaction is unique. Your positive attitude and your ability to deal with different types of people are the tools necessary to close and move into your new home. Central to every transaction is a buyer that wants the best deal and a seller that wants the best deal. Coming to a reasonable compromise is the name of the game, but realize it is not always possible. This handbook is about choices. Making proper choices requires being equipped with the right information.

This guide will help you make choices that will **SIGNIFICANTLY REDUCE MISCOMMUNICATION, MISUNDERSTANDINGS AND UNMET EXPECTATIONS.**

So without further ado, let's go through each step and by the time you make it to the end of this book, I promise you will feel better about your transaction. I am going to be frank about things in this publication and you may even find a bit of sarcasm.

I realize that my readers will vary in knowledge. Those of you who have done this before and are reasonably comfortable with the process, please bear with me. The intent of this material is not to insult anyone's intelligence, but is geared towards those who are a little anxious about their home purchase.

"HONEY, LET'S BUT A HOUSE!"

This is how it usually starts, unless you are a single buyer (and you could be, so do not be offended by the heading). The dream of owning realized. Isn't that what we all want? So you pile your friends, neighbors and disgruntled significant others into the car and take off on that search for THE HOUSE. Most of the people in the car are trying to tell you not to do it, but you insist. Before you know it you are standing on someone's property gazing lovingly at the house, seeing yourself in the yard and in the second story windows…and you still do not realize that it is not even for sale. **BACK TO REALITY PLEASE!**

THE FIRST STEP

This is what should happen before you make a decision to buy. You should ask yourself, "Why own a home?" Do you want to invest money wisely? Do you just want your own piece of the rock? Are you just tired of apartment living? Do you want to begin a family that just won't fit in the one bedroom apartment you now live in? Do you want to prove that the guy on the Infomercial was right, you know, the one who told you about owning with no money down. Search your heart. No one can tell you that your reason for wanting to own is wrong. In fact, there is probably no wrong reason for owning real property. You just need to be careful that you have weighed the advantages and the disadvantages of owning and that you are willing to deal with them all as a part of ownership. Bring in a financial advisor, accountant or your attorney if their advice would be critical to your decision.

Once you have decided that owning is the right thing for you, MAKE THE TRIP to your bank, mortgage broker, or anyone else that you think will give you the money needed to fund your real estate deal. **Yes, you will probably need money or other assets to complete the deal, no matter what that guy on television told you.** When you approach a real estate professional it is important to be able to tell them your purchase limit (your financial expert will make this clear) and expected down payment before you begin looking for the house. Without that information it is difficult for a real estate professional to help you find that perfect home.

SHOW ME THE MONEY!

These days there are many, many sources of funding available for real estate purchases. So many that most people are confused and don't know where to turn. Should they go to the bank, should they borrow from Aunt Sara? How much will they need? How much can they afford? If you are a first time home buyer, this will indeed be one of the most frightening parts of your real estate purchase. How do you know what type of funding is best for you?

Well, the first thing is to have at least a little general knowledge about what types of products are available. This handbook will provide you with general information. There are also many different types of loan programs. It will be impossible to detail all of them, even in a college course on funding. However, I will do my best to expose you to some of the most common sources. Again, this is not a complete list.

Tips For Choosing A Funding Source

You must know a little about what is required by funding sources before you decide whether to skip the bank and choose a mortgage broker. One of the most important things funding sources want to know about is your credit scores. Today there is no such thing as good credit or bad credit, just scores and history.

*Do you know what your credit report says about you?

*Do you pay your bills on time all the time?

*Have you ever filed a bankruptcy or had a judgment against you?

Your credit rating will be the foremost indicator of which organization you should head to first. Note, if you have no credit history at all (you pay everything by cash), you may be considered a high risk borrower

5

because no patterns of payments have been recorded. This can be as bad of a position as having a bad credit history. If you pay all of your bills on time you probably have a good credit history and you probably can shop anywhere. However, excessive lines of credit (having every credit card known to man), can be negatively rated even if you pay all of them on time.

If you want to learn more about your credit history, contact any major credit bureau, obtain your credit report and have a counselor explain how to read it and how to understand the overall rating. The three major credit bureaus are Equifax, TransUnion and Experian. Credit reports are obtainable via the internet too. You can compare what all three are saying about you. Once you know and understand your report, you will be able to direct your energies to a lender that can help you. It is critical for you to shop for loans and compare terms. Look for the best interest rates, application fees and loan fees.

Credit Unions provide loan products to their members only. They are very competitive with rates and may even offer a better interest rate than other commercial products. They are picky about your credit rating. If you have had trouble in the past, like 3 years ago, and have a real good explanation of late payments they may work with you. They may not look kindly upon charge-offs and judgments regardless of how much time has passed. If you have a problem area and this source of funding meets your needs, then **ASK** up front so as not to waste your time and application fee.

Banks are also another source of funding. They are competitive and may have more products to choose from than your Credit Union. Bankers like good credit loans. Some have products available for the less than perfect history. Inquire about the products available to you in regards to your credit history. NOTE: Once you have applied for a loan with a banker and more than ten days have passed, or the term "It's still in underwriting" is used flippantly, without hope of an answer, move on. I have found in the course of my work that loan officers at the bank work for the bank. Let's just say that your deal could fold before they answer and they will frankly not care.

A **mortgage company** is generally a direct source of funding. Mortgages are the primary product. They have their own products and their own set of guidelines and sometimes in-house underwriting. This means that you will get quick service and quick answers. If your credit scores fall in the A-B loan category (Excellent to Average), the mortgage company may be a good source of funding for you.

The **mortgage broker** works with many different lenders. Mortgage brokers will work with A-Z credit ratings (Excellent to Extremely Poor) because they can shop the products for you. If you have very special issues, this might be your best bet. These loan officers want to make the loan. They will work with you and help you find the best investor for your situation. Although they are very competitive sources of funding, the fees for using a mortgage broker can be slightly higher than traditional loan sources and they are less likely to offer any concessions.

First Time Home Buyer Programs you have seen advertised are great to work with too. However, many must be underwritten by specific lenders. Also, funding is based on specific criteria and guidelines. **While your agent can help you find a home that meets the guidelines, keep in mind that a seller may refuse to work with your program. These programs can add significant stipulations and time constraints that deter the seller from accepting them.**

Regardless of the type of loan provider and program you choose to work with, remember to take the time to shop for what **you** want. Many real estate agents and brokers are also loan originators or loan officers, so of course they want you to work with the company they are with. Even if they are not involved in the loan origination they may suggest you work with a company that works within their office. Why? The reason is very simple, they know how the loan officer works. This is important to your real estate professional because they (me included) like to work with a loan officer that they can actually talk to during the transaction. These loan professionals will be cordial and will communicate with your agent. If things get frustrating for you, your agent and your loan professional will work together to make sure you understand what is needed to complete your transaction.

If your loan professional is having trouble getting a piece of information from you, they can utilize our relationship by having us gently encourage you to supply what they need. A working relationship between your agent and your lender is also valuable if your file is in danger of not closing. Your agent's input can be instrumental in helping you to close your file without your lender having to disclose much information about the file. Your assets or your liabilities are important as to your ability to purchase. Therefore, your agent's communication with your loan officer does not include specifics about your financial standing. A little warning here if you don't want your real estate professional to communicate with your loan officer, you need to stay in contact with lender and be ready to provide them with all of the information required until your transaction is closed.

Keep in mind that your lender may not be in the same hurry as you are to close your home on time. The pre-qualification or pre-approval letter you were given may only mean that the information you presented to the lender was satisfactory at the time. Everything you told your lender must be supported by actual documentation which may include check stubs, bank statements, rental history, and job verifications in order for the loan to pass the final underwriting stage. Any discrepancies will be questioned and delay your final processing.

AND WE'RE OFF!

Wow! Can you believe it? You are so far ahead of the game. Now you are ready for the real fun. Either you have gotten a pre-qualification or pre-approval or you have been turned down. Regardless, it's time to move forward. Those of you who have been turned down, continue reading and then devise a credit repair plan with your lender so you can repeat THE FIRST STEP.

For the rest of you, if you are ready, let's find that house. I believe that the best way to begin a home search is to get in touch with a Real Estate professional. I am not just suggesting this because that is what I am. A real estate professional usually has access to every home listed through a multiple listing service in the city in which you live. They also have access to every listed property in your state, and other states through a network of other brokers. A real estate professional can give you good advice during your transaction. They assist you with the reading and writing all of the necessary contracts and addendum that make up your transaction.

Your real estate professional will also interact with others involved in the transaction on your behalf. All in all, your real estate professional understands the market and how it works. Even if you have three college degrees and you are perfectly capable of finding a home or investment property on your own, you probably will want to have a real estate professional or an attorney working on your behalf.

Here are a few myths about using real estate professionals:

MYTH 1: I want to buy a home listed "for sale by owner" or FSBO (that is pronounced "fisbo"), I don't want a real estate professional because the seller said they don't want one involved.

REALITY CHECK: You need to ask yourself, "Why wouldn't the seller have a professional involved?" This is one of the most important decisions of your life. How do you know if the seller is being just? If the seller tells you to present an offer, do you know where to start? How do you know if you are getting your money's worth for the property? Be careful! Many sellers in this position do not want to pay your professional's fee to sell their home even if they will have a professional represent them. The seller's agent can write the documents for you but you better find out and get in writing whose side they are on (This is called Agency Disclosure in the field). You can hire a real estate professional or an attorney or both to represent you in the transaction. The seller or the seller's agent does not protect your interests.

MYTH 2: I had a realtor that I signed an agreement with for representation. I didn't think I was being represented so I fired him. Now I am so angry, I think I will just do this myself.

REALITY CHECK: BE ANGRY, but don't let it get the best of you. Find another Realtor® or find an attorney to help you, unless again, you are not one of those people that need this book.

It is in your best interest to have someone you can trust help you with the real estate transaction. I did say someone who you can trust didn't I. All real estate agents are not made equal. The key to finding a good agent is in the method of selection. You find a good agent the same way you find a good grocery store, a good husband, a good baby sitter, a good steak or anything that meets your definition of what is good. What is good for me is not necessarily good for you. But say you respect the advice of your friend of 15 years and your friend just bought a lovely home on the lake in what looked like the easiest real estate transaction on earth. Wouldn't you take your friends advice if he recommended "Bob the BEST REALTOR® FOR THE BEST BUY?" Sure you would. You would call "Bob" (for short) and find out whether he would help you with your transaction. This is one way to find a good realtor (or attorney for that matter). It is called "Word of Mouth" or "the Referral". If you don't have any friends, you can also find a good real estate professional or attorney through their respective local boards. Many professional profiles are now available via the Internet.

Regardless of method you choose, once you are face to face with the person, check certain things out. How many years has this person been in business, what is his/her expertise? Is the person sociable or stiff necked? Are they crisp and sharp or laid back? This is subjective stuff, but you have to look at the traits that are important to you. I believe, and this is just my humble opinion, the worst way to find a real estate professional is to just walk into an office on the corner and say "Hey! I'm looking for a house." (Sorry my fellow associates, but we all know this is the truth).

You could end up with someone unsuitable for your situation or you may end up with a great agent. In any event, choose someone you are comfortable with. Maybe years of experience doesn't matter to you. Let's face it, all agents have to start somewhere. There are good first timers in this business and good old timers too. ASK QUESTIONS! Find out if the person is right for you. As you get into your transaction you will realize that your selected professional should be able to do slightly more than open the lock box to show you a home.

A LITTLE LOYALTY WOULDN'T HURT!

Now that I have given you sound advice on finding a professional to work with, a little loyalty wouldn't hurt. Real estate professionals are no different from any other professional. They want to pour their expertise into your transaction, but how is that possible when you are undermining their efforts. The truth is, we don't appreciate (I know it is strong language) buyers who think they need a different agent each time they see a cool looking house.

Your agent will usually have instant access in the office or on the road (handheld PDA's and lap tops make this possible) to any listing in the multiple listing database. Your agent can find the house you just "found".

However, that special little house is probably outside the criteria you gave your agent when you began your search. Usually the cool looking house did not appear on the list of homes diligently prepared by your agent because IT WAS NOT PART OF YOUR SPECIFICATIONS - it has 2 bedrooms, you asked for 3. It has 1 bath, you asked for 2. It is $300,000, according to your lender; your limit is $65,000. Besides all of that, it has been SOLD and the listing agent has chosen not to display this information on a sign. Do you see what is happening here?

So your agent is not lame, he/she just didn't know about your inheritance from rich Uncle Larry), nor about your desire for 2 bedrooms. However, had you specified those things, your agent could have told you that the house had already been SOLD and therefore, would have saved you and your agent a lot of time and trouble. When you signed that Buyer Representation agreement, you agreed to let your agent represent you. (Oh you haven't done this? You may think twice about that after reading the next chapter.) What good would it do your professional to hold your dream home back from you?

I would like to take a moment to dispel (MYTH #3).

MYTH 3: The agent's job is not to drive around and show you houses in a random fashion. When I began in this profession, I drove a customer around for many days with no hope of finding "The Right House." Later, after making a decision not to buy, the customer casually said, "that is your job isn't it?' Well gee, NO I don't think so. That is not my job. My job is to help you find the right home at the best price in the best condition within your ideal time frame.

There is a lot of detail that most people get very overwhelmed with in the middle of the process that also becomes "MY JOB". How would you like it if I showed the home we just wrote an offer on to several different people, then wrote up several different offers on that house, and you were bid right out of your dream house. By the way this is not illegal for me to do, but I personally see something ethically wrong with doing so.

OK, SO I TRUST YOU! WHAT'S IN IT FOR ME?

Do I Have To Sign That Thing?

I assume you are speaking of the infamous Buyer/Tenant Representation Agreement. That horrid document with the tiny writing that you think will bind you forever to some real estate professional that you don't want to work with. You want to be free. You want to take things at your own pace. **TAKE IT EASY**. The Buyer/Tenant Representation allows the real estate professional that you choose to give you undivided attention. It moves you from being just a customer to a client, someone that is taken seriously. You can ward off the advances of other real estate professionals that you don't wish to work with by telling them you have a written agreement for representation with an agent of your choice.

Instead of having to call on many differentreal estate professionals, your agent can and will do all the things that you need. When most buyers meet an agent, they are soon handed a form that is titled **"INFORMATION ABOUT BROKERAGE SERVICES"** (at least that is what it is called in Texas.) This topic is so important that I must bore you with the details of the actual form.

As you will note the form **BEGINS** with the following statement:

Before working with a real estate broker, you should know that the duties of a broker depend on whom the broker represents. If you are a prospective seller or landlord (owner) or a prospective buyer or tenant (buyer), you should know that the broker who lists the property for sale or lease is the owner's agent. A broker who acts as a subagent represents the owner in cooperation with the listing broker. A broker who acts as a buyer's agent represents the buyer. A broker may act as an intermediary between the parties if the parties consent in writing. A broker can assist you in locating a property, preparing a contract or lease, or obtaining financing without representing you. A broker is obligated by law to treat you honestly. (Exerpt from TRECOP-K)

And **ENDS** with:

If you choose to have a broker represent you, you should enter into a written agreement with the broker that clearly establishes the broker's obligations and your obligations. The agreement should state how and by whom the broker will be paid. You have the right to choose the type of representation, if any, you wish to receive. Your payment of a fee to a broker does not necessarily establish that the broker represents you. If you have any questions regarding the duties and responsibilities of the broker, you should resolve those questions before proceeding. (Exerpt from TRECOP-K)

Basically, it is highly recommended that you get the broker's position in writing. According to the "Information About Brokerage Service's" form, representation generally takes three different forms:

Case 1. If The Broker
Represents The Owner:

The broker becomes the owner's agent by entering into an agreement with the owner, usually through a written listing agreement or by agreeing to act as a subagent by accepting an offer of subagency from the listing broker. A subagent may work in a different real estate office. A listing broker or subagent can assist the buyer but does not represent the buyer and must place the interests of the owner first. (Exerpt from TRECOP-K)

Buyer's purchasing new homes give us a classic example of owner representation gone wrong. When you walk into the new home sales office and are wowed by the sales counselors, pinch yourself and remember that they represent the seller and want you to buy a new home. Your interests are not protected. They do not represent your interests as a buyer. Many buyers may find themselves in various binds after closing on a new home that could have been prevented had they entered into a written buyer's representation agreement with a real estate professional. Most people think that having a new home warranty is enough protection in case some thing goes wrong. However, many find out too late this is not the case.

Case 2. If The Broker
Represents The Buyer:

The broker becomes the buyer's agent by entering into an agreement to represent the buyer, usually through a written buyer representation agreement A buyer's agent can assist the owner but does not represent the owner and must place the interests of the buyer first.

Your signed buyer's representation agreement binds your agent to confidentiality too. Think about the seriousness of this. Let's say you decide that having an agreement is not necessary because you are business saavy. You found an agent that will work with you for FREE and the agent agrees to assist you with finding a home and preparing the paperwork. Oh, Oh. Something goes wrong after the papers are all signed. "Your Agent" as you fondly refer to him or her states that you asked for their assistance but they did not agree to represent you. You can't blame the listing agent because he has an agreement with the seller that states he exclusively represents the seller. You are on your own. The buyer's representation agreement also spells out how your professional will be paid, so there are no misunderstandings between parties.

If you are unhappy with your agent's services the relationship may be terminated, so why would you risk going into the transaction without adequate representation?

Case 3. If The Broker
Acts As An Intermediary:

A broker may act as an intermediary between the parties if the broker complies with The Texas Real Estate Licence Act. The broker must obtain the written consent of each party to the transaction to act as an intermediary. The written consent must state who will pay the broker and, in conspicuous bold or underlined print, set forth the broker's obligations as an intermediary. (Exerpt from TRECOP-K)

There are four specific things a broker who acts as an intermediary must do:

a. Treat all parties honestly
b. Get written authorization from an owner before disclosing that the owner will accept a price less than the asking price
c. Get written authorization from the buyer before disclosing that the buyer will pay a price greater than the price submitted in a written offer

    d.   Get written authorization to disclose any confidential information or any information that a party specifically instructs the broker in writing not to disclose, unless they are required to do so by The Texas Real Estate License Act for a court order or if the information materially relates to the condition of the property.

Won't an agent work with you anyway, even if you don't sign one of these agreements? Yes, there are some that will. But if they are willing to work without an agreement, how else are they willing to compromise an important part of your transaction. If they can't get you to commit to working exclusively with them, can they get a commitment from the seller on your terms? Do you want to work with someone that doesn't have the backbone to give you an agreement for providing services that they take seriously. If they take their work seriously, then won't they take every part of the transaction seriously. Think about the reasons why you won't sign an agreement and you may find that you are doing yourself more harm than good.

If I have not convinced you yet that a written and executed buyer's representation agreement is in your best interest, then here is a REAL LIFE WHAT'S IN IT FOR ME. Let's say you see an advertisement for a home and it includes a REBATE of 1% to the buyer. The agent offering the REBATE wants to work only with buyers. You decide to work with the agent but refuse to sign the buyer's representation agreement. The agent agrees to assist you with paperwork and other details of the sale. At closing, you are expecting to receive your REBATE and the agent says "sorry!" You are confused and demand that you receive the REBATE. Well, you may have a problem. According to rebate guidelines, it is only permissible for a licensee to give a rebate to a PRINCIPAL in any real estate transaction as long as the licensee obtains the consent of the person the licensee represents. The agent only agreed to assist you with paperwork, the agent did not agree to represent you. The agent owes you nothing. Do you want to reconsider signing that agreement?

So You Wanna Buy A House!

TEXAS ASSOCIATION OF REALTORS®

RESIDENTIAL BUYER/TENANT REPRESENTATION AGREEMENT

USE OF THIS FORM BY PERSONS WHO ARE NOT MEMBERS OF THE TEXAS ASSOCIATION OF REALTORS® IS NOT AUTHORIZED.
©Texas Association of REALTORS®, Inc. 2004

---

1. PARTIES: The parties to this agreement are:

Client: _____

Address: _____
City, State, Zip: _____
Phone: _____ Fax: _____
E-Mail: _____

Broker: _____
Address: _____
City, State, Zip: _____
Phone: _____ Fax: _____
E-Mail: _____

2. APPOINTMENT: Client grants to Broker the exclusive right to act as Client's real estate agent for the purpose of acquiring property in the market area.

3. DEFINITIONS:
   A. *"Acquire"* means to purchase or lease.
   B. *"Closing"* in a sale transaction means the date legal title to a property is conveyed to a purchaser of property under a contract to buy. "Closing" in a lease transaction means the date a landlord and tenant enter into a binding lease of a property.
   C. *"Market area"* means that area in the State of Texas within the perimeter boundaries of the following areas: _____
   _____
   _____

   D. *"Property"* means any interest in real estate including but not limited to properties listed in a multiple listing service or other listing services, properties for sale by owners, and properties for sale by builders.

4. TERM: This agreement commences on _____ and ends at 11:59 p.m. on _____ .

5. BROKER'S OBLIGATIONS: Broker will:
   A. use Broker's best efforts to assist Client in acquiring property in the market area;
   B. assist Client in negotiating the acquisition of property in the market area; and
   C. comply with other provisions of this agreement.

6. CLIENT'S OBLIGATIONS: Client will:
   A. work exclusively through Broker in acquiring property in the market area and negotiate the acquisition of property in the market area only through Broker;
   B. inform other brokers, salespersons, sellers, and landlords with whom Client may have contact that Broker exclusively represents Client for the purpose of acquiring property in the market area and refer all such persons to Broker; and
   C. comply with other provisions of this agreement.

(TAR-1501) 7-7-04   Initialed for Identification by: Broker/Associate _____ , and Client _____ , _____   Page 1 of 4

The Texas Buyer's Broker 5850 San Felipe, Suite 500, Houston TX 77057
Phone: 713-270-4616   Fax: Corinne Luna   Book.zfx
Produced with ZipForm™ by RE FormsNet, LLC 18025 Fifteen Mile Road, Clinton Township, Michigan 48035 www.zipform.com

19

Corinne T. Luna

Buyer/Tenant Representation Agreement between _____

7. REPRESENTATIONS:
A. Each person signing this agreement represents that the person has the legal capacity and authority to bind the respective party to this agreement.
B. Client represents that Client is not now a party to another buyer or tenant representation agreement with another broker for the acquisition of property in the market area.
C. Client represents that all information relating to Client's ability to acquire property in the market area Client gives to Broker is true and correct.
D. Name any employer, relocation company, or other entity that will provide benefits to Client when acquiring property in the market area: _____ .

8. INTERMEDIARY: *(Check A or B only.)*

☐ A. Intermediary Status: Client desires to see Broker's listings. If Client wishes to acquire one of Broker's listings, Client authorizes Broker to act as an intermediary and Broker will notify Client that Broker will service the parties in accordance with one of the following alternatives.
   (1) If the owner of the property is serviced by an associate other than the associate servicing Client under this agreement, Broker may notify Client that Broker will: (a) appoint the associate then servicing the owner to communicate with, carry out instructions of, and provide opinions and advice during negotiations to the owner; and (b) appoint the associate then servicing Client to the Client for the same purpose.
   (2) If the owner of the property is serviced by the same associate who is servicing Client, Broker may notify Client that Broker will: (a) appoint another associate to communicate with, carry out instructions of, and provide opinions and advice during negotiations to Client; and (b) appoint the associate servicing the owner under the listing to the owner for the same purpose.
   (3) Broker may notify Client that Broker will make no appointments as described under this Paragraph 8A and, in such event, the associate servicing the parties will act solely as Broker's intermediary representative, who may facilitate the transaction but will not render opinions or advice during negotiations to either party.

☐ B. No Intermediary Status: Client does not wish to be shown or acquire any of Broker's listings.

Notice: **If Broker acts as an intermediary under Paragraph 8A, Broker and Broker's associates:**
   ♦ **may not disclose to Client that the seller or landlord will accept a price less than the asking price unless otherwise instructed in a separate writing by the seller or landlord;**
   ♦ **may not disclose to the seller or landlord that Client will pay a price greater than the price submitted in a written offer to the seller or landlord unless otherwise instructed in a separate writing by Client;**
   ♦ **may not disclose any confidential information or any information a seller or landlord or Client specifically instructs Broker in writing not to disclose unless otherwise instructed in a separate writing by the respective party or required to disclose the information by the Real Estate License Act or a court order or if the information materially relates to the condition of the property;**
   ♦ **shall treat all parties to the transaction honestly; and**
   ♦ **shall comply with the Real Estate License Act.**

9. COMPETING CLIENTS:
Client acknowledges that Broker may represent other prospective buyers or tenants who may seek to acquire properties that may be of interest to Client. Client agrees that Broker may, during the term of this agreement and after it ends, represent such other prospects, show the other prospects the same properties that Broker shows to Client, and act as a real estate broker for such other prospects in negotiating the acquisition of properties that Client may seek to acquire.

10. CONFIDENTIAL INFORMATION:
During the term of this agreement or after its termination, Broker may not knowingly disclose information obtained in confidence from Client except as authorized by Client or required by law. Broker may not disclose to Client any information obtained in confidence regarding any other person Broker represents or may have represented except as required by law.

(TAR-1501) 7-7-04   Initialed for Identification by: Broker/Associate _____ , and Client _____ , _____   Page 2 of 4

Produced with ZipForm™ by RE FormsNet, LLC 18025 Fifteen Mile Road, Clinton Township, Michigan 48035 www.zipform.com   Book.zfx

20

Buyer/Tenant Representation Agreement between _____

11. BROKER'S FEES:

A. **Commission:** The parties agree that Broker will receive a commission calculated as follows:
(1) _____ % of the gross sales price if Client agrees to purchase property in the market area; and
(2) if Client agrees to lease property in the market a fee equal to (check only one box): ☐ _____ %
of one month's rent or ☐ _____ % of all rents to be paid over the term of the lease.

B. **Source of Commission Payment:** Broker will seek to obtain payment of the commission specified in Paragraph 11A first from the seller, landlord, or their agents. If such persons refuse or fail to pay Broker the amount specified, Client will pay Broker the amount specified less any amounts Broker receives from such persons.

C. **Earned and Payable:** A person is not obligated to pay Broker a commission until such time as Broker's commission is *earned and payable*. Broker's commission is earned when: (1) Client enters into a contract to buy or lease property in the market area; or (2) Client breaches this agreement. Broker's commission is *payable*, either during the term of this agreement or after it ends, upon the earlier of: (1) the closing of the transaction to acquire the property; (2) Client's breach of a contract to buy or lease a property in the market area; or (3) Client's breach of this agreement. If Client acquires more than one property under this agreement, Broker's commissions for each property acquired are earned as each property is acquired and are payable at the closing of each acquisition.

D. **Additional Compensation:** If a seller, landlord, or their agents offer compensation in excess of the amount stated in Paragraph 11A (including but not limited to marketing incentives or bonuses to cooperating brokers) Broker may retain the additional compensation in addition to the specified commission. Client is not obligated to pay any such additional compensation to Broker.

E. **Acquisition of Broker's Listing:** Notwithstanding any provision to the contrary, if Client acquires a property listed by Broker, Broker will be paid in accordance with the terms of Broker's listing agreement with the owner and Client will have no obligation to pay Broker.

F. In addition to the commission specified under Paragraph 11A, Broker is entitled to the following fees.
(1) **Construction:** If Client uses Broker's services to procure or negotiate the construction of improvements to property that Client owns or may acquire, Client ensures that Broker will receive from Client or the contractor(s) at the time the construction is substantially complete a fee equal to:
_____
(2) **Service Providers:** If Broker refers Client or any party to a transaction contemplated by this agreement to a service provider (for example, mover, cable company, telecommunications provider, utility, or contractor) Broker may receive a fee from the service provider for the referral.
(3) **Other:** _____
_____
_____

G. **Protection Period:** "Protection period" means that time starting the day after this agreement ends and continuing for _____ days. Not later than 10 days after this agreement ends, Broker may send Client written notice identifying the properties called to Client's attention during this agreement. If Client or a relative of Client agrees to acquire a property identified in the notice during the protection period, Client will pay Broker, upon closing, the amount Broker would have been entitled to receive if this agreement were still in effect. This Paragraph 11G survives termination of this agreement. This Paragraph 11G will not apply if Client is, during the protection period, bound under a representation agreement with another broker who is a member of the Texas Association of REALTORS® at the time the acquisition is negotiated and the other broker is paid a fee for negotiating the transaction.

H. **Escrow Authorization:** Client authorizes, and Broker may so instruct, any escrow or closing agent authorized to close a transaction for the acquisition of property contemplated by this agreement to collect and disburse to Broker all amounts payable to Broker.

I. **County:** Amounts payable to Broker are to be paid in cash in _____ County, Texas.

(TAR-1501) 7-7-04   Initialed for Identification by: Broker/Associate _____ , and Client _____ , _____   Page 3 of 4

Produced with ZipForm™ by RE FormsNet, LLC 18025 Fifteen Mile Road, Clinton Township, Michigan 48035 www.zipform.com   Book.zfx

21

Corinne T. Luna

12. MEDIATION: The parties agree to negotiate in good faith in an effort to resolve any dispute that may arise related to this agreement or any transaction related to or contemplated by this agreement. If the dispute cannot be resolved by negotiation, the parties will submit the dispute to mediation before resorting to arbitration or litigation and will equally share the costs of a mutually acceptable mediator.

13. DEFAULT: If either party fails to comply with this agreement or makes a false representation in this agreement, the non-complying party is in default. If Client is in default, Client will be liable for the amount of compensation that Broker would have received under this agreement if Client was not in default. If Broker is in default, Client may exercise any remedy at law.

14. ATTORNEY'S FEES: If Client or Broker is a prevailing party in any legal proceeding brought as a result of a dispute under this agreement or any transaction related to this agreement, such party will be entitled to recover from the non-prevailing party all costs of such proceeding and reasonable attorney's fees.

15. LIMITATION OF LIABILITY: Neither Broker nor any other broker, or their associates, is responsible or liable for Client's personal injuries or for any loss or damage to Client's property that is not caused by Broker. Client will hold broker, any other broker, and their associates, harmless from any such injuries or losses. Client will indemnify Broker against any claims for injury or damage that Client may cause to others or their property.

16. ADDENDA: Addenda and other related documents which are part of this agreement are:
- ☒ Information About Brokerage Services
- ☐ Protecting Your Home from Mold
- ☐ Information Concerning Property Insurance
- ☐
- ☐ Protect Your Family from Lead in Your Home
- ☐ Information about Special Flood Hazard Areas
- ☐ For Your Protection: Get a Home Inspection
- ☐

17. SPECIAL PROVISIONS: _____
_____
_____
_____

18. ADDITIONAL NOTICES:

A. **Broker's fees and the sharing of fees between brokers are not fixed, controlled, recommended, suggested, or maintained by the Association of REALTORS® or any listing service.**

B. **Broker's services are provided without regard to race, color, religion, national origin, sex, disability or familial status.**

C. **Broker is not a property inspector, surveyor, engineer, environmental assessor, or compliance inspector. Client should seek experts to render such services in any acquisition.**

D. **If Client purchases property, Client should have an abstract covering the property examined by an attorney of Client's selection, or Client should be furnished with or obtain a title policy.**

E. **Buyer may purchase a residential service contract. Buyer should review such service contract for the scope of coverage, exclusions, and limitations. The purchase of a residential service contract is optional. There are several residential service companies operating in Texas.**

F. **Broker cannot give legal advice. This is a legally binding agreement. READ IT CAREFULLY. If you do not understand the effect of this agreement, consult your attorney BEFORE signing.**

Broker's Printed Name	License No.	Client	Date

By: _____

Broker's Associate's Signature	Date	Client	Date

Produced with ZipForm™ by RE FormsNet, LLC 18025 Fifteen Mile Road, Clinton Township, Michigan 48035 www.zipform.com   Book.zfx

YOU FIND "IT"

You Have Found It! Yippee! Let's move in. Not so fast. Now the fun begins. Executing the contract, processing the loan, completing the inspections, clearing the loan conditions, and going to closing.

IF YOU ARE PAYING WITH YOUR OWN CASH, ONLY TIME STANDS BETWEEN YOU AND YOUR DREAM. IF YOU ARE DEPENDING ON SOMEONE ELSE'S CASH, THERE ARE A LOT OF FACTORS THAT STAND BETWEEN YOU AND YOUR DREAM.

For the sake of simplicity, the remaining chapters will focus on the purchase of a previously lived in home (resale purchase). If your actual purchase will be a new home, condominium, town home or unimproved land, the logistics will be a little different.

THE OFFER

You (or you as represented by your agent or attorney) will now prepare your offer after careful analysis of the market and after seeing the property. You present it to the seller and expect a positive response. You know what you want and you have done your homework. They should accept the offer without a hitch, right?

Wrong! Don't forget that the seller (in most cases) has done exactly what you have. They have done their homework. They know what they want and feel that you are being unreasonable. Although you have the right to make an offer on whatever terms you like, I don't believe in insulting a seller. That only creates tension and animosity. For instance, if I have led a client to a home, and it reasonably represents the market, I believe that the offer should represent that.

However, there are many valid reasons for not offering a full price to a seller such as really poor condition of the property. Negotiation will generally produce a good compromise. An offer to purchase will usually be made on the contract forms, however, an offer is NEVER a contract until the seller agrees to the terms and signs the offer. Beware of verbal promises. The rule of thumb is **GET IT IN WRITING.**

THE CONTRACT

This is a very important item. You cannot purchase without one and it is vitally important that you understand what is contained in your contract and what the dates in the contract mean. All contracts will have some similar items and these are the ones that I will mention as they pertain to 1-4 family resale real estate purchase contracts in Texas. I chose Texas because I am a Broker in Texas and I operate under Texas laws.

To comment on real estate contracts in other states would be inappropriate. If you are not purchasing in Texas, however, some of these items will appear somewhere in a contract no matter where it is written. All I am trying to do here is to educate you about pursuing the purchase of your dream home, earning a Ph.D. in real estate law is not our goal.

The Sales Price

This is the price you agree to pay the seller for the house. This price can change during the course of the transaction. One common reason for the sales price to change is because the appraised market value of the house is lower than the sales price.

The Down Payment

This is the amount your loan officer has told you will be required to obtain your loan. These amounts are generally fixed at 3%, 5%, 10% or 20% of the total sales price. You may put down more than the minimum required, but make sure your loan officer is informed of this plan. **Do not get this amount confused with closing costs.**

Your estimated closing costs will include the down payment but consists of many other costs. Customary fees that are a part of closing costs are fees related to obtaining your loan, prepaid taxes, interest and insurance, fees related to your title policy, messenger and courier fees, and attorney fees just to name a few. **Your down payment plus these fees make up your TOTAL closing costs.** That is why when "No Money Down" is stated in an advertisement, **it never means you won't have any money coming out of your pocket**. It may simply mean that 100% financing may be obtained under the advertised circumstances, but it does not mean that there will not be any other closing costs involved.

Amount Financed

This is the difference between the sales price and the down payment. It is the amount that the bank will actually finance. Sometimes there are premiums added to this that will be calculated later such as the FHA mortgage insurance premium (if you are getting an FHA loan).

Financing Source

There are different addendum (forms added to the contract that address specific details of the sale) for different types of funding. Your real estate professional will know which one to use based on your financing. This is another great reason for pre-approval. If during the course of the transaction your loan officer decides that FHA financing would be better for you than a conventional loan the contract must be re-written to accommodate the changes. Note that a change in financing may affect the seller's closing costs and if the seller refuses the change in financing you may find that you are out of contract.

Title Company (Escrow Officer)

The Title Company is the holder of the "earnest money" if your contract is written with earnest money. In Texas, earnest money is not required to add validity to your contract, however, the seller may not give you the time of day without it. It may be viewed as your earnest interest in purchasing the property. The Title Company will also normally handle the title search and close the sale.

An attorney can also act as escrow officer and close your sale. The Buyer can choose the Title Company or Escrow officer, however it is not untypical for the Seller to choose. You will find this to be a negotiable item on the contract. Generally, if the seller is going to be particular about this, they will state it up front. Also, note that the agency that holds the escrow does not have to be the same company that provides the title policy.

Survey

Your lender or the title company will normally order a survey of the property. This document is important because it tells you where the legal boundaries of your property begin and end. It also tells you the limits of easements and whether there are underground pipelines that you should be aware of. Once the survey is available, you have the right to ask the lender or title company to review it and be satisfied with it prior to closing. The time to handle the pipeline running through the center of the property is definitely before closing. Many homeowners do not check the survey until something goes wrong. When something goes wrong it is going to come out of someone's pocket.

Seller's Disclosure

This is a document that the seller has completed which details the items that the seller is knowledgeable about that are attached to the property, that come with the property, that happened to the property or that has been repaired or treated on the property. ***Do not rely on this document to forgo an inspection.***

Property Condition

The details of the property condition that is acceptable to you is probably the most confusing, necessary and misunderstood section of the contract. The buyer is stating here that they "accept the property in its present condition, provided the Seller at the Sellers expense, shall complete the following specific repairs and treatments". Then there is a space provided for you to fill out what you want. The trouble with this section is that in many instances, the Buyer does not know what, if anything needs repair, because the need for repairs may not be obvious. In some cases the repairs may be obvious. If you are purchasing a home that was previously owned, there may be repairs necessary even if it is noted that the owner took exceptional care of the home.

My suggestion, especially in the case of a previously owned home is to focus on things that would render the home uninhabitable, unsafe and unsanitary. The replacement of a light bulb stated in a contract would most

---

Quoted from the Texas Real Estate Commission promulgated 1 - 4 family form, item 7(d)

likely irritate even the most conscientious seller and seriously embarrass your agent who has to present this thing (your offer). It is an entirely different story if the electrical wires leading to the light fixture are fried or not there. Do you get my drift? Again this is a touchy area, but being realistic is the key.

Residential Service Contracts

Residential service contracts, sometimes referred to as Home Warranties can be an important item to have. These contracts provide some assurance that items such as plumbing, electrical, HVAC, pools, termites, and appliances (not an all inclusive list as each warranty is different), which were included with your purchase can be repaired or replaced if necessary for a nominal fee. Your contract states that the Buyer can purchase such a contract and the Seller will reimburse the Buyer at closing up to an amount that the Buyer specifies. If you want one, be sure that this section is not left blank. Review different warranties to find one best suited to your needs.

Closing Date & Possession

This is a very important topic. In this day of technological advancement, closings can happen as early as 5-10 days after the contract has been signed and placed in escrow. You do not need to rush this process. There will be factors in your life that may affect this date such as the ending of your current lease term or the sale of your current home. A typical time frame for a closing is 30-45 days. Possession of the property typically occurs on the date the sale has closed and funded (all money has changed hands). Sometimes the buyer needs to move in earlier or sometimes the seller needs more time to move. In either of these cases you need to put in writing what you mean. I never think it is a good idea for the buyer to move in early nor for the seller to stay later, but these situations do occur. My advice is to make sure you specify the conditions of any such occurrences and treat them as a legal transaction or you may be in for a few unwanted surprises.

Special Provisions

This will contain only the facts about the sale that cannot be handled by another addendum.

Notices

This section of the contract details the buyer's information and the seller's information. This information is used to send important correspondence to the buyer and seller during the transaction.

Settlement and Other Expenses

This section is being brought to your attention because it provides a list of normal closing costs a Buyer or a Seller would pay. Additional expenses that the Seller has been asked to pay towards Buyer's expenses must be written in for the Seller to be liable for that amount.

Agreement of Parties

This section lists all the addenda that are a part of the contract. An addendum is a document that has been made a part of the contract and has business details that will pertain to the sale. For instance, a Non-Realty Addendum can be made a part of the contract if both buyer and seller agree that a washer and dryer will be made a part of the sale.. An addendum will be added to the contract as deemed necessary by your real estate professional. If the title of the addendum is not on the pre-printed list, then your agent must add it to the "Other" section. An addendum that is part of your contract must be listed as such or technically, it does not exist as part of the contract.

Termination Option

A Buyer may purchase an unrestricted right to terminate the contract with an option fee. Unrestricted simply means even if your dog dies you can terminate the contract, but note that you will lose your option fee. Your earnest money, however, will be refunded. If you do not terminate the contract within the specified time, you are obligated to the terms of the contract. The option fee can be credited to the Sales Price at closing if the buyer continues with the sale. Yes, you may do inspections during your option period, but your findings do not obligate the seller to make any repairs to the property per your inspection. Repairs requested during an option period that were not part of the original agreement call for the renegotiating of the contract if you wish to continue with the purchase. **DO NOT ASSUME THAT THE SELLER WILL TAKE CARE OF ANY REPAIRS ONCE YOU CAN PROVE THAT THE HOUSE IS FALLING TO THE GROUND.**

Consult an Attorney

If the Buyer or the Seller has retained an attorney to assist with the sale, the attorney's information would be provided in this section.

Effective Date & Signatures

The effective date of the contact is the date that both parties (Buyer and Seller) came to an agreement. This date is not necessarily the date that the physical document is signed. As soon as the seller accepts the offer and notifies the Buyer of such Acceptance, the contract is effective. This date can be filled in by either agent and will drive all of the other details that must occur within specified days throughout the contract. The contract must be signed by both parties to be a binding document. (Make sure your real estate professional delivers a copy of this document to you.)

Sellers Receipt

The Seller will complete this section if there is an Option Fee involved. If the Option Fee is not properly exchanged, (The contract states "Buyer has paid Seller (amount) (option fee) for the unrestricted right to terminate contract by giving notice of termination to Seller within (# days) after the effective date of this contract."), the validity of the option period may be affected.

Brokerage Information

This section details the amount of commission that will be paid to the Buyer's Broker by the Seller's Broker. It also contains the business information for the Selling and Listing Agents in the transaction. There are separate agreements that determine what will be written here. They are the Buyer's Representation agreement between the Buyer and the buyer's agent and the Listing Agreement between the Seller and the seller's agent.

Escrow Receipt

The Title Company will complete this section to record the date they received earnest money (if any) from the buyer. Your earnest money should be turned into the escrow officer within 2 days of the effective date of your contract.

In summary, there is no question that is stupid when it comes to the contract. If there is anything within the contract that you don't understand, you have the right to obtain a satisfactory answer from your agent.

READ YOUR CONTRACT. IF YOU STILL HAVE QUESTIONS AFTER READING YOUR CONTRACT AND THIS MATERIAL, ASK!

Of course I could not detail every word of the contract, but I have tried to provide you with some of the highlights. Just as every property is different so will every contract be different for each sale. There is no such thing as a cookie cutter deal.

WINDING IT UP OR DOWN

Yippee!!! I've got an accepted contract...I've got an accepted contract (can you hear the music?). **NOW WHAT?**

Well, if you are buying a home in "as-is" condition with CASH, then closing is next. If not, (perhaps the majority of cases) there will be Inspections, Appraisals, and Surveys (Oh my)! Let's not forget about satisfying your loan conditions. No one on earth can prepare you for this process, but I am going to certainly try.

PATIENCE IS DEFINITELY REQUIRED. FOLLOWING INSTRUCTIONS DOESN'T HURT EITHER.

First of all, there are people that need to get this contract. You need a copy, your lender needs a copy, the escrow agent (or title company), the seller and the agents involved. The lender begins to finalize your loan, the title company begins to prepare documents for your title insurance, you need to begin to perform your duties under the contract and the seller begins to perform duties under the contract.

As you prepare for closing a number of things are going on behind the scenes with all parties to the transaction. Communication between all those involved becomes a necessity. Here are some common things that occur before you will close your sale.

YOU WILL COMPLETE YOUR INSPECTIONS. It is not recommended that this part be skipped. If you choose to skip inspections, don't be surprised if your agent asks you to sign a waiver. Inspection of the structure, the mechanical systems, and the grounds for wood destroying insects should be performed by a licensed inspector.

You may select an inspector of your choice from the yellow pages or any other source you deem reliable (See the chapter on Finding Your Agent as many of the same rules apply). I do not recommend using an inspector chosen by the seller because of the obvious conflict of interest. If you ask your agent to recommend an inspector, and the agent actually obliges you, then don't sue your agent if something goes wrong. You are not under obligation to use an inspector suggested by anyone. This applies to all vendors that are recommended by your agent because you insisted on a referral. If you are too lazy to do your own footwork, then don't complain about the outcome or the rates.

The cost for inspection services varies. I encourage you to shop around for the best price for the best service. Compare rates, compare services. Choose one and remember they work for you. Be present at the inspection if at all possible. Your agent can attend inspections with you or for you, however, it is not protocol for them to ask the inspector any questions concerning the inspection or make comments to you about the inspection.

OK! You choose to do inspections (a very wise choice). People that waive their right to do this are usually A) buying a new or fairly new home (still a bad choice not to do an inspection), B) inspectors themselves and all systems are go, C) cheap, D) crazy. Please do not waive your inspection because you are under the influence of C or D.

After the inspections are complete, you will be presented with reports that indicate what repairs or treatments (if any) are necessary. Please note that the inspector looks at the home according to specific guidelines and in accordance with today's building codes. If the home was built in 1955, of course the report is going to be loaded with things, that according to today's code, should be repaired or brought up to date. If you are applying for a VA or FHA loan, this may be a concern. If not, the information is provided for you to determine the inhabitability, safety, and sanitary conditions of the home. If you have bought an option and are performing the inspection during the option period, the inspection can help you determine whether you want to continue with the sale or not.

Inspections should not be performed because you think your lender will stop the sale if the findings are not satisfactory. Depending on the type of loan you are getting, the lender providing your financing may not care about what your report says. I know that is a little disappointing, but the reason you spent all of that money was to make sure you knew what your were getting into.

Meanwhile, back at the mortgage company, and at some point before closing, your lender will order an **APPRAISAL REPORT**. This report will reveal some important things such as A) Is the house worth the price stated on your contract, B) are there major issues that need to be addressed like the fault line running through the middle of the property which has substantially contributed to the 12 inch crack in the slab. This kind of stuff will be important to the lender before they give you the money.

Let's address the issue of valuation first. If the house "does not appraise" or in layman's terms if the price that you agreed upon with the seller is higher than the formal appraisal, then the house "did not appraise." A couple of things can happen at this point, you can try to re-negotiate the price based on the appraisal or it is possible that the contract may terminate. You will not get funding until the price has come down to meet the appraisal. Under some circumstances it may be frugal to pay the difference - for instance you want the home so bad you are willing to pay more than it is worth to have it. I don't think this is smart, but what do I know? The seller will probably not like what has happened, but the choice for them is "Sell" or wait for the next buyer and a new appraisal. The probability for a new appraisal which quickly follows to come out very different from the first is slim. I didn't say it was impossible. It may be in the best interest of the seller to re-negotiate at this point, *WE HOPE*.

This brings up the issue of **LENDER REQUIRED REPAIRS**. What are these anyway? They are things that the Lender requires to be repaired in order to complete processing of your loan. The appraisal is usually the document that makes the lender require repairs before they will give money. These repairs commonly involve problems that will make the house fall into the ground and seriously damage the resale value of the property at some future date if not taken care of now. Cracked foundations, bad roofs and termites are just a few of the common lender required repairs and treatments.

I want to point out here that if for some reason your financing source chooses not to do an appraisal (and this sometimes happens) the seller may not have a duty to repair what you think is a "lender required repair." Just calling an issue with the property a lender required repair or treatment does not make it a lender required repair or treatment.

THE LENDER MUST REQUIRE IT AND USUALLY WILL NOTIFY THE BUYER AND SELLER (if it is indeed a lender required repair or treatment) IN WRITING.

Closing Time

Your reports have come in and they look great, that is the Inspection, Appraisal, and Survey. Whew! That was a lot of work! You are at the closing table. Everyone is smiling (hopefully). You have the money, the property appraised, any requested repairs or required ones are complete, you want your property and you want it now!

Okay....what can go wrong at closing?

1. No one told you to get INSURANCE. Yes, you will need insurance to close the deal. I suggest you look into getting some right after your contract is signed. Choose any insurance company you wish and yes, you will be charged a whole years premium plus 2-3 months for your escrow account (that is if you are required to have one).

2. The psychedelic lamp in the kitchen does not stay. As you and the seller are engaged in small talk at the table, you find out that they are planning to take that really fab psychedelic lamp. You thought it was a part of the deal. You are not going to sign the papers because you want that lamp. The seller won't sign cause he is taking it. Hopefully this will never happen because your carefully selected agent would have made sure you were informed of items excluded from the purchase and those items would be additionally spelled out in writing on your contract.

3. What do you mean I can't move in until next week? You remember that paragraph in your contract that talked about possession? You better make sure that the seller is on the same page about moving their stuff out and you moving yours in. If there are going to be special circumstances, don't take anyone's word for it. Get it in writing!

4. I am not paying for that stupid warranty! Oops! The title company made an error and put this charge on your side. They make mistakes too. Just calmly state that the seller said he would pay and they will check the contract and move the item to the seller's side, saving the day! By the way, it is an extremely good idea for you or your agent to obtain the Settlement Statement (sometimes referred to as the HUD-1) at least 24 hours before closing. This is not just a good idea, but you have the right to review it prior to closing.

No one can anticipate and stop every situation that could occur at the closing table from happening, but there are a quite a few that can be halted with proper preparation and honest communication between all parties. *You have managed to obtain the keys, your agent is exhausted....now go and enjoy your home. When you are ready to sell, call your agent and get ready to experience the other side of the transaction.*

ABOUT CORINNE

Corinne Luna is a licensed Real Estate Broker and Mortgage Broker in the State of Texas. She holds a Masters Degree in Business Administration from Houston Baptist University, and a Bachelors of Science Degree in Psychology from the University of Houston. She is married to John Luna Jr. and they have three children, Tish, Amanda and Marissa and one grandchild Ahlauna.

TABLE OF CONTENTS

ES USTED se PREPARA?

Decidí escribir esta guía después que trabajando con muchos compradores que estaban nerviosos acerca del proceso. Por mucho detalló la explicación de lo que transpiraría durante la transacción, ellos tendrían una mirada asustada en sus caras completamente a la mesa final. Creo que esa ansiedad de comprador se relaciona directamente confiar. Permitanos la cara, comprando una casa es una inversión financiera mayor. Hacer tal inversión para la primera vez adicionalmente estresante.

Las cosas bárbaros lejos, la transacción total es un casamiento de tipos entre extranjeros completos. Cada transacción de bienes raíces es extraordinaria. Su actitud positiva y su habilidad de tratar con tipos diferentes de personas son los instrumentos necesarios para cerrar y cambiarse a su casa nuevo. Central a cada transacción es un comprador que quiere el mejor trato y a un vendedor que quiere el mejor trato. La venida a un arreglo razonable es el objeto, pero se da cuenta de no es siempre posible. Esta guía está acerca de elecciones. Hacer las elecciones apropiadas requieren a ser equipado con la información correcta.

Esta guía lo ayudará a hacer las elecciones que **REDUCEN APRECIABLEMENTE** la **MALA COMUNICACION**, la **EQUIVOCACION Y las ESPERANZAS INAPROPIADAS.**

Así que sin la actividad adicional, atravesemos cada paso y cuando usted hace lo al fin de este libro, yo prometo que usted se sentirá mejor acerca de su transacción. Seré franco acerca de cosas en esta publicación y usted puede aún hallazgo un poco de sarcasmo.

Yo me doy cuenta de que mis lectores variarán en el conocimiento y para los que han hecho esto antes y son razonablemente cómodo con el proceso, por favor oso conmigo. La intención de esta materia no deberá insultar nadie inteligencia, pero se engrana verdaderamente hacia los que son un poco ansioso acerca de su compra de casa.

¡ *"Amor vamos a compra una casa!"*

Esto es cómo empieza generalmente, a menos que usted sea un solo comprador (y usted podría ser, así que no es ofendido por el título). El sueño de poseer se dio cuenta de. ¿Eso no es lo que todos nosotros necesidad? Así que usted amontona a sus amigos, los vecinos y los otros significativos contrariado en el coche y toma lejos en esa búsqueda para LA CASA. La mayor parte de las personas en el coche tratan de decirlo no hacerlo, pero usted insiste. Antes usted lo sabe usted se para en alguien la propiedad que mira adorar en la casa, viéndose en la yarda y en las segundas ventanas del cuento…Y usted todavía no se da cuenta de que es ni en venta. **¡APOYE A la REALIDAD POR FAVOR!**

EL PRIMER PASO

Esto es lo que debe suceder antes usted se toma un decisión de comprar. ¿Debe preguntarse usted, "por qué posee una casa?" ¿Quiere usted invertir dinero sabiamente? ¿Usted acaba de querer su propio pedazo de la piedra? ¿Usted acaba de cansars de vivir de apartamento? ¿Quiere usted empezar una familia que apenas no quedará en el un apartamento de dormitorio que usted ahora vive en? Hágalo quiere demostrar que el tipo en el Infomercial tenía razón, usted sabe, el que lo dijo acerca de poseer sin dinero hacia abajo. Busque el corazón. Nadie puede decir usted que su razón para querer para poseer está equivocado. De hecho, probablemente no hay la razón equivocada para poseer la propiedad verdadera. Usted acaba de necesitar para tener cuidado que usted ha pesado las ventajas y las desventajas de poseer y que usted está dispuesto a tratar con ellos todo como una parte de la propiedad. Introduzca a un consejero financiero, el contable o su abogado si su consejo sería crítico a su decisión.

Una vez que usted ha decidido que ese poseer es la cosa correcta para usted, HACE EL VIAJE a su banco, a corredor de hipoteca, o a cualquiera más que usted piensa le dará el dinero necesitó financiar su trato de bienes raíces. **Sí, usted necesitará probablemente dinero u otras ventajas para completar el trato, ningún asunto lo que ese tipo en la televisión lo dijo.** Cuándo usted se acerca a un profesional de bienes raíces es importante ser capaz de decirles su límite de compra (su experto financiero hará este vacía) y desembolso inicial esperado antes usted comienza a buscar la casa. Sin esa información es difícil que un profesional de bienes raíces ayudelo a encontrar que eso perfecciona en casa.

Mí Muestran El Dinero

Estos días hay muchos, muchos fondo provisto disponible para compras de bienes raíces. Tanto que la mayoría de las personas son confundidas y no saben donde girar. ¿Deben ir ellos al banco, deben ellos piden prestados de la Tía Sara? ¿Cuánto ellos necesitarán? ¿Cuánto ellos pueden proporcionar? Si usted es un primer tiempo en casa comprador, esto será verdaderamente uno de partes más espantosas de su compra de bienes raíces. ¿Cómo sabe usted qué tipo de la financiación es mejor para usted?

Bien, la primera cosa deberá tener por lo menos una cultura general pequeña acerca de qué tipos de productos está disponible. Esta guía lo proporcionará con información general. Hay también muchos tipos diferentes de programas de préstamo. Será imposible detallar todo ellos, aún en un curso colegial en la financiación. Sin embargo, yo haré mi exponérselo mejor a algunos de fuentes más comunes. Otra vez, esto no es una lista completa.

Las PUNTAS PARA ESCOGER UNA FUENTE de la FINANCIACION

Usted debe saber un pequeño acerca de lo que es requerido financiando las fuentes antes usted decide si saltarse el banco y escoger a un corredor de la hipoteca. Uno de las cosas más importantes que financia las fuentes quiere saber acerca de es sus cuentas del crédito. Hoy no existe el crédito bueno o el crédito malo, apenas cuentas e historia.

¿Sabe usted lo que su informe de crédito dice acerca de usted?

¿Paga usted sus cuentas a la hora todo el tiempo?

¿Ha archivado jamás usted una insolvencia o tenido un juicio contra usted?

Su calificación del crédito será el indicador primero de cuál la organización usted debe dirigir a primero. La nota, si usted tiene no historia del crédito en todo (usted paga el todo por el dinero efectivo), usted puede ser considerado a un prestatario alto del riesgo porque ningunas pautas de pagos se han registrado. Esto puede ser como malo de una posición teniendo como una historia mala del crédito. Si usted paga todas sus cuentas a la hora usted tiene probablemente una historia buena del crédito y usted puede hacer de compras probablemente dondequiera. Sin embargo, línea de crédito excesiva (teniendo cada tarjeta de crédito conocida al hombre), puede ser valorado negativamente incluso si usted pagado todo ellos a la hora.

Si usted quiere aprender más acerca de su historia de crédito, contactar oficina mayor del crédito, obtener su informe del crédito y tener a un consejero explica para cómo leerlo y cómo entender la calificación general.

Las tres oficinas mayores del crédito son Equifax, TransUnion y Experian. Los informes del crédito son que se pueden conseguir en linea vía el internet también. Usted puede comparar lo que todo tres dicen acerca de usted. Una vez que usted sabe y entiende su informe, usted será capaz de dirigir sus energías a un prestamista que puede ayudar usted. Es crítico para usted hacer de compras para préstamos y comparar los términos. Busque los mejores tipos de interés, los honorarios de la aplicación y honorarios de préstamo.

Las unión de crédito proporcionan el préstamo los productos a sus miembros sólo. Ellos son muy competitivos con tasas y pueden aún oferta un mejor tipo de interés que otros productos comerciales. Ellos son seleccionados acerca de su calificación del crédito. Si usted ha tenido el problema en el pasado, como hace 3 años, y tiene una explicación buena verdadera de tarde pagos que ellos pueden trabajar con usted. Ellos no pueden mirar amablemente sobre carga lejos y los juicios a pesar de cómo mucho veces ha pasado. Si usted tiene un asunto problemático y este fondo provisto satisface sus necesidades, entonces **PREGUNTAN** arriba la frente por no perder el tiempo y el honorario de la aplicación.

Los bancos son también otro fondo provisto. Ellos son competitivos y pueden tener más productos para escoger de que su unión de crédito. Los banqueros quieren el crédito que bueno presta. Algunos tienen los productos disponibles para el menos que perfecciona la historia. Pregunte acerca de los productos disponibles a usted con respecto a su historia de crédito. La NOTA: una vez usted ha solicitado un préstamo con un banquero y más de diez días ha pasado, o el término "Es todavía en el seguro" es utilizado ligeramente, sin la esperanza de una respuesta, mueve en. Yo encontrado en el curso de mi trabajo que presta los oficiales en el trabajo bancario trabajan para el banco. Digamos apenas que su trato podría doblar antes ellos contestan y ellos francamente no cuidarán.

Una **compañía de la hipoteca** es generalmente un fondo provisto directo. Las hipotecas son el producto primario. Ellos tienen sus propios productos y su propio conjunto de pautas y seguro a veces interno. Esto significa que usted obtendrá el servicio rápido y las respuestas rápidas. Si su caída de cuentas de crédito en la UNA categoría del préstamo B (Excelente Promediar), la compañía de la hipoteca puede ser un fondo provisto bueno para usted.

El **corredor de la hipoteca** trabaja con muchos prestamistas diferentes. Los corredores de la hipoteca trabajarán con UNA calificaciones del crédito Z (Excelente a Muy Pobre) porque ellos pueden hacer de compras los productos para usted. Si usted tiene los asuntos muy especiales, esto quizás sea su mejor apuesta. Estos prestan a oficiales quieren hacer el préstamo. Ellos trabajarán con usted y lo ayudan a encontrar al mejor inversionista para su situación. Aunque ellos sean el fondo provisto muy competitivos, los honorarios para utilizar a un corredor de la hipoteca puede ser las fuentes levemente más alto que tradicionales del préstamo y ellos son menos probable de ofrecer cualquier concesión.

Primero Tiempo en casa Comprador lo Programa ha visto anunciado son gran trabajar con también. Sin embargo, muchos deben ser asegurados por prestamistas específicos. También, la financiación se basa en criterios y pautas específicos. **Mientras su agente lo puede ayudar a encontrar una casa que encuentra las pautas, tenga presente que un vendedor puede negar a trabajar con su programa. Estos programas pueden agregar limitaciones significativas de estipulaciones y tiempo que disuaden al vendedor de los aceptar.**

A pesar del tipo de proveedor de préstamo y lo programa escoge trabajar con, para recordar de tomar el tiempo de hacer de compras para lo **que usted quiere**. Muchos agentes de bienes raíces y corredores son también autores de préstamo u oficiales de préstamo, así que por supuesto ellos quieren que usted trabaje con la compañía que ellos están con. Incluso si ellos no sean implicados en el principio del préstamo que ellos pueden sugerir que usted trabaja con una compañía que trabaja dentro de su oficina. ¿Por qué? La razón es muy sencilla, ellos saben cómo los trabajo de oficial de préstamo. Esto es importante a su profesional de bienes raíces porque ellos (mí incluí) como trabajar con un oficial del préstamo que ellos pueden hablar verdaderamente a durante la transacción. Estos prestan a profesionales serán cordial y comunicarán con su agente. Si las cosas obtienen frustrando para usted, su agente y su profesional del préstamo trabajarán juntos para cerciorarselo entiende lo que se necesita completar su transacción.

Si su profesional del préstamo tiene el problema que obtiene un pedazo de información de usted, ellos pueden utilizar nuestra relación teniéndonos suavemente lo alentamos a suministrar lo que ellos necesitan. Una relación de trabajo entre su agente y su prestamista es también valiosa si su archivo corre peligro de no cerrar. Su entrada del agente puede ser instrumental en lo ayudando a cerrar su archivo sin su prestamista para tener que revelar mucha información acerca del archivo. Sus ventajas o sus obligaciones son importantes en cuanto a su habilidad de comprar. Por lo tanto, su comunicación de agente con su oficial del préstamo no incluye específico

Acerca de su posición financiera. Una advertencia pequeña aquí si usted no quiere que su profesional de bienes raíces comunique con su oficial del préstamo, usted necesita permanecer en el contacto con prestamista y estar listo para proporcionarlos con toda la información requerida hasta que su transacción se cierre.

Tenga presente que su prestamista no puede estar en el mismo apuro como usted deberá cerrar su casa a la hora. El del requisito pre o de la carta de la aprobación pre que usted se dieron pueden sólo medio que la información usted presentó al prestamista era satisfactorio en el tiempo. El todo usted dijo a su prestamista debe ser sostenido por la documentación verdadera que puede incluir talonarios de cheques, los estados del banco, la historia de la renta, y comprobaciones de trabajo en la orden para el préstamo para pasar la etapa de suscripción final. Cualquier discrepancia se preguntará y demorará su procesamiento final.

¡Y ESTAMOS APAGADOS!

¡Ah! ¿Lo puede creer usted? Usted es hasta ahora adelante del juego. Ahora usted está listo para la diversión verdadera. O usted ha obtenido un del requisito pre o de la aprobación pre o usted ha sido rechazado. Pese a, es tiempo de adelantarse. Los que han sido rechazados, continúan la lectura y entonces idean un plan de la reparación del crédito con su prestamista tan usted puede repetir EL PRIMER PASO.

Para el resto de usted, si usted está listo, permitanos el hallazgo que alberga. Creo que la mejor manera de empezar una búsqueda de casa deberá ponerse en contacto con un profesional de bienes raíces. Yo no sugiero apenas este porque eso es lo que soy. Un profesional de bienes raíces tiene acceso generalmente a cada casa listó por un múltiplo que lista el servicio en la ciudad en que usted vive. Ellos tienen acceso también a cada listó la propiedad en su estado, y en otros estados por una red de otros corredores. Un profesional de bienes raíces le puede dar consejo bueno durante su transacción. Ellos lo ayudan con la lectura y escribiendo todos los contratos y el apéndice necesarios que componen su transacción.

Su profesional de bienes raíces actuará recíprocamente también con otros implicados en la transacción en su beneficio. Todo en total, su profesional de bienes raíces entiende el mercado y cómo trabaja. Incluso si usted tenga tres grados colegiales y usted es perfectamente capaz de encontrar una propiedad de casa o inversión en su propio, usted querrá probablemente tener un profesional de bienes raíces o un abogado que trabajan en su beneficio.

Aquí están unos pocos mitos acerca de utilizar a profesionales de bienes raíces:

El MITO 1: quiero comprar una casa listó "en venta por dueño" o FSBO (eso se pronuncía "fisbo"), yo no quiero a un profesional de bienes raíces porque el vendedor dijo que ellos no quieren un implicado.

¿El CHEQUE de la REALIDAD: necesita preguntarse, "por qué hace Usted no el vendedor tiene a un profesional implicado?" Esto es uno de decisiones más importantes de su vida. ¿Cómo sabe usted si el vendedor es apenas? ¿Si el vendedor lo dice presentar una oferta, usted sabe donde empezar? ¿Cómo sabe usted si usted obtiene su valor de dinero para la propiedad? ¡Tenga cuidado! Muchos vendedores en esta posición no quieren pagar su honorario de profesional por vender su casa incluso si ellos tendrán a un profesional los representa. El agente del vendedor puede escribir los documentos para usted pero para usted averigua mejor y entra escritura cuyo lado ellos están en (Esto se llama la Agencia la Revelación en el campo). Usted puede emplear un profesional de bienes raíces o a un abogado o ambos representarlo en la transacción. El vendedor o el agente del vendedor no protegen sus intereses.

El MITO 2: tuve a un corredor de bienes raíces que firmé un acuerdo con para la representación. Yo no pensé que era representado tan yo lo despedí. Ahora estoy tan enojado, pienso que acabo de hacer este yo mismo.

El CHEQUE de la REALIDAD: ESTA ENOJADO, pero no permitió aventajar para alo. Encuentre a otro Corredor de bienes raíces o encuentre a un abogado para ayudarlo, a menos que otra vez, usted no sea uno de esas personas que necesitan este libro.

Está en su mejor interés de tener alguien usted puede confiar ayuda usted con la transacción de bienes raíces. Dije que alguien que usted puede confiar hizo no yo. Todos agentes de bienes raíces no son hechos iguales. La llave a encontrar a un agente bueno está en el método de la selección. Usted encuentra a un agente bueno la misma manera usted encuentra una abarrotería buena, un marido bueno, una baby sitter buena de bebé, un filete bueno o algo que encuentra su definición de lo que son buenos. Qué es bueno para mí no es necesariamente muy bien. Pero dice que usted respeta el consejo de su amigo de 15 años y su amigo compró apenas una casa encantador en el lago en lo que se pareció a la transacción más fácil de bienes raíces en la tierra. ¿No tomaría usted su consejo de amigos si él recomendó "Bob al MEJOR CORREDOR DE BIENES RAICES® PARA EL COMPRA MEJOR?" Seguro usted hace. Usted llamaría "Bob" (para corto) y averigua si él lo ayudaría con su transacción. Esto es una manera de encontrar a un corredor de bienes raíces bueno (o el abogado en cuanto a eso). Se llama "Palabra de Boca" o "la Referencia". Si usted no tiene a ningún amigo, usted puede encontrar también un profesional bueno de bienes raíces ni a abogado por sus tablas locales respectivas. Muchos perfiles profesionales están ahora disponibles vía en linea el Internet.

A pesar del método que usted escoge, una vez que usted es la cara para encarar con la persona, verifica ciertas cosas fuera. ¿Cuántos años tienen a esta persona estuvo en el negocio, qué es su pericia? ¿La persona es necked social o tiesa? ¿Ellos son espaldas curruscantes y agudas o colocadas? Esto es el material subjetivo, pero usted tienen que mirar los rasgos que son importantes a usted. ¡Creo, y esto es apenas mi opinión humilde, la peor manera de encontrar que un profesional de bienes raíces deberá andar apenas en una oficina en el rincón y decir "Oye! Busco una casa." (Arrepentidos mis socios de hombre, pero todos saben que esto es la verdad).

Usted podría acabar por con alguien inapropiado para su situación o usted puede acabar por con un gran agente. En todo caso, escoge alguien usted es cómodo con. Quizá años de la experiencia no importan a usted. Permitanos la cara, todos agentes tienen que empezar en algún lugar. Hay bueno primero relojes en este negocio y relojes viejos buenos también. ¡HAGA PREGUNTAS! Averigüe si la persona tiene razón para usted. Cuando usted entra en su transacción usted se dará cuenta de que su profesional escogido debe ser capaz de hacer levemente más que abierta la caja de la cerradura para mostrarle una casa.

¡UNA LEALTAD PEQUEÑA no DOLERIA!

Ahora que yo le he dado consejo sano a encontrar a un profesional a trabajar con, una lealtad pequeña no dolería. Los profesionales de bienes raíces son no diferente de cualquier otro profesional. Ellos quieren vertir su pericia en su transacción, pero cómo es que posible cuando usted socava sus esfuerzos. La verdad es, nosotros no apreciamos (sé es el idioma fuerte) compradores que piensan que ellos necesitan a un agente diferente cada vez ellos ven una casa fresca que mira.

Su agente tendrá generalmente el acceso instantáneo en la oficina o en el camino (las cimas portátiles de PDA y regazo hacen este posible) a cualquier lista en la base de datos de la lista del múltiplo. Su agente puede encontrar la casa que usted acaba de "encontrar".

Sin embargo, esa casa pequeña especial es probablemente fuera de los criterios usted dio a su agente cuando usted empezó su búsqueda. Generalmente la casa fresca que mira que no apareció en la lista de casaes diligentemente preparado por su agente porque no ERA la PARTE DE SUS ESPECIFICACIONES - tiene 2 dormitorios, usted pidió 3. Tiene 1 baño, usted pidió 2. Es $300,000, según su prestamista; su límite es $65,000. Además todo eso, se HA VENDIDO y el agente de la lista ha escogido no demostrar esta información en un signo. ¿Ve usted lo que sucede aquí?

Así que su agente no es cojo, él/ella apenas no supo acerca de su herencia del Tío rico Larry), ni acerca de su deseo para 2 dormitorios. Sin embargo, lo tuvo especificó esas cosas, su agente podría haber dicho usted que la casa ya HABIA SIDO VENDIDA y por lo tanto, lo habría salvado y su mucho tiempo de agente y problema. Cuándo usted firmó ese acuerdo de la Representación de Comprador, usted concordó en permitir que su agente lo represente. ¿ (Ah usted no ha hecho esto? Usted puede pensar dos veces acerca de que después de leer el próximo capítulo.) ¿Qué bueno haría lo a su profesional para tener su sueño en casa espalda de usted?

Querría tomar un momento de disipar (el MITO #3).

El MITO 3: El trabajo de agente no deberá manejar alrededor de y mostrar usted alberga en una moda aleatoria. Cuándo yo empecé en esta profesión, yo manejé a un cliente alrededor por muchos días sin la esperanza del hallazgo "La Casa Correcta." ¿Más tarde, después que tomándose un decisión de no comprar, el cliente dijo casualmente, "eso es su trabajo no es?' Bien caramba, no creo que no. Eso no es mi trabajo. Mi trabajo lo deberá ayudar a encontrar el casa correcto en el mejor precio en la mejor condición dentro de su agenda ideal.

Hay mucho detalle que la mayoría de las personas obtienen muy agobiado con en el centro del proceso que llega a ser también "MI TRABAJO". Cómo hágalo como lo si mostré el casa que acabamos de escribir una oferta en a varias personas diferentes, entonces aumento de valor varias ofertas diferentes en esa casa, y usted era el derechos de la oferta fuera de su casa de sueño. Por la manera que esto no es ilegal para mí hacer, pero veo personalmente algo éticamente injusticia con hacer así.

¡BUENO, ASI QUE yo LO CONFIO!

¿Que Es En Ello Para Mi?

Asumo que usted habla del Comprador de mala fama/el Acuerdo de la Representación de Arrendatario. Ese documento horrible con la escritura diminuta que usted piensa lo atará para siempre a algún profesional de bienes raíces que usted no quiere para trabajar con. Usted quiere ser libre. Usted quiere tomar las cosas en su propio ritmo. **TOMELO FACIL**. El Comprador/la Representación de Arrendatario permite al profesional de bienes raíces que usted escoge darle atención indivisa. Lo mueve de es apenas un cliente a un cliente, alguien que es tomado gravemente. Usted puede desvía los avances de otros profesionales de bienes raíces que usted no desea para trabajar con diciendolos usted tiene un acuerdo escrito para

La representación con un agente de su elección.

En vez de tener que visitar muchos diferentelos profesionales de bienes raíces, su agente puede Y hará todas las cosas que usted necesita. Cuándo la mayoría de los compradores encuentran a un agente, ellos pronto son entregados una forma que se titular La "INFORMATION ABOUT BROKERAGE SERVICES" (por lo menos eso es qué se llama en Tejas). "Este tema es tan importante que deba Abúrralo con una detalles de la forma verdadera.

Cuando usted notará que la forma EMPIEZA con la declaración siguiente: :

Antes trabajar con un corredor de bienes raíces, usted debe saber que los deberes de un corredor dependen de quien el corredor representa. Si usted es un vendedor o el propietario (dueño) prospectivo o un comprador o el arrendatario (comprador) prospectivo, usted debe saber que el corredor que lista la propiedad en venta o el arrendamiento son el agente de dueño. Un corredor que actúa como un subagent representa al dueño en la cooperación con el corredor de la lista. Un corredor que actúa como un agente de comprador representa al comprador. Un corredor puede actuar como a un intermediario entre los partidos si los partidos consienten en la escritura. Un corredor lo puede ayudar a localizar una propiedad, preparando un contrato o el arrendamiento, u obteniendo el financiamiento sin representarlo. Un corredor es obligado por la ley a tratarlo honestamente. (Exerpt de TRECOP K)

Y los FINES con:

Si usted escoge tener un corredor lo representa, usted debe entrar en un acuerdo escrito con el corredor que establece claramente las obligaciones de corredor y sus obligaciones. El acuerdo debe indicar cómo y por quien el corredor será pagado. Usted tiene el derecho de escoger el tipo de la representación, si cualquiera, usted desea recibir. Su pago de un honorario a un corredor no establece necesariamente que el corredor lo representa. Si usted tiene cualquiera pregunta considerando los deberes y responsabilidades del corredor, usted debe resolverse esas preguntas antes de avanzar. (Exerpt de TRECOP K)

Básicamente, se recomienda sumamente que usted obtiene la posición de corredor en la escritura. Según la "Información acerca de Forma de Servicio" de Correduría, la representación toma generalmente tres formas diferentes:

Caso 1. Si El Corredor Representa A Dueño:

El corredor llega a ser el agente de dueño entrando en un acuerdo con el dueño, generalmente por un acuerdo escrito de lista o concordando en actuar como un subagent aceptando una oferta de subagency del corredor de la lista. Un subagent puede trabajar en una oficina diferente de bienes raíces. Un corredor de la lista o subagent pueden ayudar al comprador pero no representar al comprador y deben colocar los intereses del dueño primero. (Exerpt de TRECOP K)

El comprador de casas nuevos compradores nos dan un ejemplo clásico de la representación de dueño falló. Cuándo usted anda en la oficina nueva de ventas la casa y es enloquecido por los consejeros de ventas, se pellizca y recuerda que ellos representan al vendedor y quieren que usted compre una casa nuevo. Sus intereses no se protegen. Ellos no representan sus intereses como un comprador. Muchos comprador puede encontrar a sí mismo en varios lazos después que cerrar en la casa nuevo que se pudiera haber prevenido tuvo ellos entraron en un acuerdo escrito de la representación de comprador con un profesional de bienes raíces. La mayoría de las personas piensan que eso teniendo una garantía nueva de casa es suficiente protección en caso de que alguna cosa falle. Sin embargo, muchos averiguan también tarde que esto no es el caso.

Caso 2. Si El Corredor
Representa A El Comprador:

El corredor llega a ser el agente de comprador entrando en un acuerdo para representar al comprador, generalmente por un acuerdo escrito de representación de comprador UN agente de comprador puede ayudar al dueño pero no representar al dueño y debe colocar los intereses del comprador primero.

Su firmó el acuerdo de la representación de comprador ata a su agente a la confidencialidad también. Piense acerca de la seriedad de esto. Digamos que usted decide que eso teniendo un acuerdo no es necesario porque usted es saavy de negocio. Usted encontró a un agente que trabajará con usted para LIBRE y el agente concuerda en ayudarlo con encontrar la casa y preparar el papeleo. Ah, Ah. Algo falla después que los papeles que todo se firman. "Su Agente" como usted se refiere cariñosamente a él o ella indica que usted pidió su ayuda pero ellos no concordaron en representarlo. Usted no puede culpar al agente de la lista porque él tiene un acuerdo con el vendedor que indica él representa exclusivamente al vendedor. Usted es solo. El acuerdo de la representación del comprador deletrea también cómo su profesional será pagado, así que no hay las equivocaciones entre partidos.

¿Si usted es infeliz con sus servicios de agente que la relación se puede terminar, así que por qué arriesgaría para entrar usted la transacción sin la representación adecuada?

Caso 3. Si El Corredor
Actua Como A Un Intermediario:

Un corredor puede actuar como a un intermediario entre los partidos si el corredor se conforma con El Acto de la Licencia de bienes raíces de Tejas. El corredor debe obtener el consentimiento escrito de cada partido a la transacción para actuar como a un intermediario. El consentimiento escrito debe indicar quién pagará al corredor y, en la impresión visible, brava o subrayada, expuso las obligaciones de corredor como un intermediario. (Exerpt de TRECOP K)

Hay cuatro cosas específicas un corredor que actúa como a un intermediario debe hacer:

a. Trate todos partidos honestamente

b. Obtenga la autorización escrita de un dueño antes revelar que el dueño aceptará un precio menos que el precio de oferta

c. Obtenga la autorización escrita del comprador antes revelar que del comprador pagará un precio más que el precio se sometió en una oferta escrita

d. Obtenga la autorización escrita para revelar información confidencial o información que un partido instruye específicamente al corredor en la escritura para no revelar, a menos que ellos sean requeridos a hacer así por El Acto de la Licencia de bienes raíces de Tejas para una orden del tribunal o si la información relaciona materialmente a la condición de la propiedad.

¿No trabajará un agente con usted de todos modos, incluso si usted no firmará uno de estos acuerdos? Sí, hay algún que hace. Pero si ellos están dispuestos a trabajar sin un acuerdo, cuán son más ellos dispuesto a ceder una parte importante de su transacción. ¿Si no lo pueden obtener ellos cometer a trabajar exclusivamente con ellos, ellos pueden obtener un compromiso del vendedor en sus términos? Hágalo quiere trabajar con alguien que no tiene el elemento principal para darle un acuerdo para proporcionar los servicios que ellos toman gravemente. Si ellos toman su trabajo gravemente, entonces hace no ellos toman cada parte de la transacción gravemente. Piense acerca de las razones por qué usted no firmará un acuerdo y usted puede encontrar que usted se hace más daña que bueno.

Si yo no lo he convencido mas que un escrito y ejecutado el acuerdo de la representación de comprador está en su mejor interés, entonces aquí está una DE LA VIDA REAL CUÁL ESTÁ EN ÉL PARA MÍ. Digamos que usted ve un anuncio para la casa e incluye un REEMBOLSO de 1% al comprador. El agente que ofrece el REEMBOLSO quiere trabajar sólo con compradores. Usted decide trabajar con el agente pero el desecho para firmar el acuerdo de la representación de comprador. El agente concuerda en ayudarlo con papeleo y otros detalles de la venta. ¡En el fin, usted espera recibir su REEMBOLSO y el agente dice "arrepentido!" Usted es confundido y demanda que usted recibe el REEMBOLSO. Bien, usted puede tener un problema. Según reembolsar las pautas, son sólo permisible para un concesionario para dar un reembolso a un DIRECTOR en cualquier transacción de bienes raíces tan largo como el concesionario obtiene el consentimiento de la persona que el concesionario representa. El agente sólo concordó en ayudarlo con papeleo, el agente no concordó en representarlo. El agente le debe nada. ¿Quiere usted volver a considerar firmar ese acuerdo?

TEXAS ASSOCIATION OF REALTORS®

RESIDENTIAL BUYER/TENANT REPRESENTATION AGREEMENT

USE OF THIS FORM BY PERSONS WHO ARE NOT MEMBERS OF THE TEXAS ASSOCIATION OF REALTORS® IS NOT AUTHORIZED.
©Texas Association of REALTORS®, Inc. 2004

1. **PARTIES:** The parties to this agreement are:

   Client: _____
   _____
   Address: _____
   City, State, Zip: _____
   Phone: _____ Fax: _____
   E-Mail: _____

   Broker: _____
   Address: _____
   City, State, Zip: _____
   Phone: _____ Fax: _____
   E-Mail: _____

2. **APPOINTMENT:** Client grants to Broker the exclusive right to act as Client's real estate agent for the purpose of acquiring property in the market area.

3. **DEFINITIONS:**
   A. *"Acquire"* means to purchase or lease.
   B. *"Closing"* in a sale transaction means the date legal title to a property is conveyed to a purchaser of property under a contract to buy. "Closing" in a lease transaction means the date a landlord and tenant enter into a binding lease of a property.
   C. *"Market area"* means that area in the State of Texas within the perimeter boundaries of the following areas: _____
   _____
   _____
   _____

   D. *"Property"* means any interest in real estate including but not limited to properties listed in a multiple listing service or other listing services, properties for sale by owners, and properties for sale by builders.

4. **TERM:** This agreement commences on _____ and ends at 11:59 p.m. on _____ .

5. **BROKER'S OBLIGATIONS:** Broker will:
   A. use Broker's best efforts to assist Client in acquiring property in the market area;
   B. assist Client in negotiating the acquisition of property in the market area; and
   C. comply with other provisions of this agreement.

6. **CLIENT'S OBLIGATIONS:** Client will:
   A. work exclusively through Broker in acquiring property in the market area and negotiate the acquisition of property in the market area only through Broker;
   B. inform other brokers, salespersons, sellers, and landlords with whom Client may have contact that Broker exclusively represents Client for the purpose of acquiring property in the market area and refer all such persons to Broker; and
   C. comply with other provisions of this agreement.

(TAR-1501) 7-7-04   Initialed for Identification by: Broker/Associate _____ , and Client _____ , _____   Page 1 of 4

The Texas Buyer's Broker 5850 San Felipe, Suite 500, Houston TX 77057
Phone: 713-270-4616   Fax: Corinne Luna   Book.zfx
Produced with ZipForm™ by RE FormsNet, LLC 18025 Fifteen Mile Road, Clinton Township, Michigan 48035 www.zipform.com

64

Buyer/Tenant Representation Agreement between _____

7. REPRESENTATIONS:
    A. Each person signing this agreement represents that the person has the legal capacity and authority to bind the respective party to this agreement.
    B. Client represents that Client is not now a party to another buyer or tenant representation agreement with another broker for the acquisition of property in the market area.
    C. Client represents that all information relating to Client's ability to acquire property in the market area Client gives to Broker is true and correct.
    D. Name any employer, relocation company, or other entity that will provide benefits to Client when acquiring property in the market area: _____ .

8. INTERMEDIARY: *(Check A or B only.)*

☐ A. Intermediary Status: Client desires to see Broker's listings. If Client wishes to acquire one of Broker's listings, Client authorizes Broker to act as an intermediary and Broker will notify Client that Broker will service the parties in accordance with one of the following alternatives.
    (1) If the owner of the property is serviced by an associate other than the associate servicing Client under this agreement, Broker may notify Client that Broker will: (a) appoint the associate then servicing the owner to communicate with, carry out instructions of, and provide opinions and advice during negotiations to the owner; and (b) appoint the associate then servicing Client to the Client for the same purpose.
    (2) If the owner of the property is serviced by the same associate who is servicing Client, Broker may notify Client that Broker will: (a) appoint another associate to communicate with, carry out instructions of, and provide opinions and advice during negotiations to Client; and (b) appoint the associate servicing the owner under the listing to the owner for the same purpose.
    (3) Broker may notify Client that Broker will make no appointments as described under this Paragraph 8A and, in such event, the associate servicing the parties will act solely as Broker's intermediary representative, who may facilitate the transaction but will not render opinions or advice during negotiations to either party.

☐ B. No Intermediary Status: Client does not wish to be shown or acquire any of Broker's listings.

Notice: **If Broker acts as an intermediary under Paragraph 8A, Broker and Broker's associates:**
    ♦ **may not disclose to Client that the seller or landlord will accept a price less than the asking price unless otherwise instructed in a separate writing by the seller or landlord;**
    ♦ **may not disclose to the seller or landlord that Client will pay a price greater than the price submitted in a written offer to the seller or landlord unless otherwise instructed in a separate writing by Client;**
    ♦ **may not disclose any confidential information or any information a seller or landlord or Client specifically instructs Broker in writing not to disclose unless otherwise instructed in a separate writing by the respective party or required to disclose the information by the Real Estate License Act or a court order or if the information materially relates to the condition of the property;**
    ♦ **shall treat all parties to the transaction honestly; and**
    ♦ **shall comply with the Real Estate License Act.**

9. COMPETING CLIENTS: Client acknowledges that Broker may represent other prospective buyers or tenants who may seek to acquire properties that may be of interest to Client. Client agrees that Broker may, during the term of this agreement and after it ends, represent such other prospects, show the other prospects the same properties that Broker shows to Client, and act as a real estate broker for such other prospects in negotiating the acquisition of properties that Client may seek to acquire.

10. CONFIDENTIAL INFORMATION: During the term of this agreement or after its termination, Broker may not knowingly disclose information obtained in confidence from Client except as authorized by Client or required by law. Broker may not disclose to Client any information obtained in confidence regarding any other person Broker represents or may have represented except as required by law.

(TAR-1501) 7-7-04   Initialed for Identification by: Broker/Associate _____ , and Client _____ _____   Page 2 of 4

Produced with ZipForm™ by RE FormsNet, LLC 18025 Fifteen Mile Road, Clinton Township, Michigan 48035 www.zipform.com   Book.zfx

65

11. BROKER'S FEES:

A. <u>Commission</u>: The parties agree that Broker will receive a commission calculated as follows:
(1) _____ % of the gross sales price if Client agrees to purchase property in the market area; and
(2) if Client agrees to lease property in the market a fee equal to (check only one box): ❑ _____ %
of one month's rent or ❑ _____ % of all rents to be paid over the term of the lease.

B. <u>Source of Commission Payment</u>: Broker will seek to obtain payment of the commission specified in
Paragraph 11A first from the seller, landlord, or their agents. If such persons refuse or fail to pay Broker
the amount specified, Client will pay Broker the amount specified less any amounts Broker receives from
such persons.

C. <u>Earned and Payable</u>: A person is not obligated to pay Broker a commission until such time as Broker's
commission is *earned and payable*. Broker's commission is earned when: (1) Client enters into a contract
to buy or lease property in the market area; or (2) Client breaches this agreement. Broker's commission
is *payable*, either during the term of this agreement or after it ends, upon the earlier of: (1) the closing of
the transaction to acquire the property; (2) Client's breach of a contract to buy or lease a property in the
market area; or (3) Client's breach of this agreement. If Client acquires more than one property under this
agreement, Broker's commissions for each property acquired are earned as each property is acquired
and are payable at the closing of each acquisition.

D. <u>Additional Compensation</u>: If a seller, landlord, or their agents offer compensation in excess of the amount
stated in Paragraph 11A (including but not limited to marketing incentives or bonuses to cooperating
brokers) Broker may retain the additional compensation in addition to the specified commission. Client is
not obligated to pay any such additional compensation to Broker.

E. <u>Acquisition of Broker's Listing</u>: Notwithstanding any provision to the contrary, if Client acquires a property
listed by Broker, Broker will be paid in accordance with the terms of Broker's listing agreement with the
owner and Client will have no obligation to pay Broker.

F. In addition to the commission specified under Paragraph 11A, Broker is entitled to the following fees.
(1) <u>Construction</u>: If Client uses Broker's services to procure or negotiate the construction of
improvements to property that Client owns or may acquire, Client ensures that Broker will receive
from Client or the contractor(s) at the time the construction is substantially complete a fee equal to:

_____

(2) <u>Service Providers</u>: If Broker refers Client or any party to a transaction contemplated by this
agreement to a service provider (for example, mover, cable company, telecommunications provider,
utility, or contractor) Broker may receive a fee from the service provider for the referral.
(3) <u>Other</u>: _____
_____
_____ .

G. <u>Protection Period</u>: "Protection period" means that time starting the day after this agreement ends and
continuing for _____ days. Not later than 10 days after this agreement ends, Broker may send Client
written notice identifying the properties called to Client's attention during this agreement. If Client or a
relative of Client agrees to acquire a property identified in the notice during the protection period, Client
will pay Broker, upon closing, the amount Broker would have been entitled to receive if this agreement
were still in effect. This Paragraph 11G survives termination of this agreement. This Paragraph 11G will
not apply if Client is, during the protection period, bound under a representation agreement with another
broker who is a member of the Texas Association of REALTORS® at the time the acquisition is
negotiated and the other broker is paid a fee for negotiating the transaction.

H. <u>Escrow Authorization</u>: Client authorizes, and Broker may so instruct, any escrow or closing agent
authorized to close a transaction for the acquisition of property contemplated by this agreement to collect
and disburse to Broker all amounts payable to Broker.

I. <u>County</u>: Amounts payable to Broker are to be paid in cash in _____ County, Texas.

(TAR-1501) 7-7-04   Initialed for Identification by: Broker/Associate _____ , and Client _____ , _____   Page 3 of 4

Produced with ZipForm™ by RE FormsNet, LLC 18025 Fifteen Mile Road, Clinton Township, Michigan 48035 www.zipform.com   Book.zfx

66

12. MEDIATION: The parties agree to negotiate in good faith in an effort to resolve any dispute that may arise related to this agreement or any transaction related to or contemplated by this agreement. If the dispute cannot be resolved by negotiation, the parties will submit the dispute to mediation before resorting to arbitration or litigation and will equally share the costs of a mutually acceptable mediator.

13. DEFAULT: If either party fails to comply with this agreement or makes a false representation in this agreement, the non-complying party is in default. If Client is in default, Client will be liable for the amount of compensation that Broker would have received under this agreement if Client was not in default. If Broker is in default, Client may exercise any remedy at law.

14. ATTORNEY'S FEES: If Client or Broker is a prevailing party in any legal proceeding brought as a result of a dispute under this agreement or any transaction related to this agreement, such party will be entitled to recover from the non-prevailing party all costs of such proceeding and reasonable attorney's fees.

15. LIMITATION OF LIABILITY: Neither Broker nor any other broker, or their associates, is responsible or liable for Client's personal injuries or for any loss or damage to Client's property that is not caused by Broker. Client will hold broker, any other broker, and their associates, harmless from any such injuries or losses. Client will indemnify Broker against any claims for injury or damage that Client may cause to others or their property.

16. ADDENDA: Addenda and other related documents which are part of this agreement are:
☒ Information About Brokerage Services   ☐ Protect Your Family from Lead in Your Home
☐ Protecting Your Home from Mold   ☐ Information about Special Flood Hazard Areas
☐ Information Concerning Property Insurance   ☐ For Your Protection: Get a Home Inspection
☐ _____   ☐ _____

17. SPECIAL PROVISIONS: _____
_____
_____
_____

18. ADDITIONAL NOTICES:

A. Broker's fees and the sharing of fees between brokers are not fixed, controlled, recommended, suggested, or maintained by the Association of REALTORS® or any listing service.

B. Broker's services are provided without regard to race, color, religion, national origin, sex, disability or familial status.

C. Broker is not a property inspector, surveyor, engineer, environmental assessor, or compliance inspector. Client should seek experts to render such services in any acquisition.

D. If Client purchases property, Client should have an abstract covering the property examined by an attorney of Client's selection, or Client should be furnished with or obtain a title policy.

E. Buyer may purchase a residential service contract. Buyer should review such service contract for the scope of coverage, exclusions, and limitations. The purchase of a residential service contract is optional. There are several residential service companies operating in Texas.

F. Broker cannot give legal advice. This is a legally binding agreement. READ IT CAREFULLY. If you do not understand the effect of this agreement, consult your attorney BEFORE signing.

_____   _____   _____   _____
Broker's Printed Name   License No.   Client   Date

By: _____   _____   _____
Broker's Associate's Signature   Date   Client   Date

USTED LO ENCUENTRA

¡Usted Lo Ha Encontrado! ¡Yippee! Movamos en. No tan rapidamente. Ahora la diversión empieza. Ejecutar el contrato, procesando el préstamo, completando las inspecciones, vaciando el préstamo condiciona, y yendo al fin.

SI USTED ESTÁ PAGANDO CON SU PROPIO EFECTIVO, SÓLO EL TIEMPO ESTÁ PARADO ENTRE USTED Y SU SUEÑO. SI USTED ES DEPENDIENDO ALGÚN OTRO EFECTIVO, HAY MUCHOS DE LOS FACTORES QUE ESTÁN PARADOS ENTRE USTED Y SU SUEÑO

Por la sencillez, los capítulos restantes enfocarán en la compra de un previamente vivido en en casa (la compra de la reventa). Si su compra verdadera será la casa nuevo, condominio, el pueblo en casa o la tierra de unimproved, la logística será un poco diferente.

LA OFERTA

Usted (o usted representó como por su agente o el abogado) ahora preparará su oferta después del análisis cuidadoso del mercado y después de ver la propiedad. Usted lo presenta al vendedor y espera una respuesta positiva. Usted sabe lo que usted quiere y usted ha hecho sus deberes. ¿Deben aceptar ellos que la oferta sin un ata, el derecho?

¡La injusticia! No olvídese que el vendedor (en la mayoría de los casos) ha hecho exactamente lo que usted tiene. Ellos han hecho sus deberes. Ellos saben lo que ellos quieren y se sienten que usted es es desrazonable. Aunque usted tenga el derecho de hacer una oferta en cualquier términos usted como, yo no creo a insultar a un vendedor. Eso sólo crea la tensión y la animosidad. Por ejemplo si he dirigido a un cliente a una casa, y a representa razonablemente el mercado, yo creo que la oferta debe representar eso.

Sin embargo, hay muchas razones válidas para no le ofrecer un precio sin descuento a un vendedor la condición tal como realmente pobre de la propiedad. La negociación producirá generalmente un arreglo bueno. Una oferta para comprar será hecho generalmente en las formas del contrato, sin embargo, una oferta es nunca un contrato hasta que el vendedor concuerde a los términos y firme la oferta. Tenga cuidado con promesas verbales. La regla empírica es **LO OBTIENE EN ESCRITURA**.

EL CONTRATO

Esto es un artículo muy importante. Usted no puede comprar sin uno y es esencialmente importante que usted entienda lo que se contiene en su contrato y en lo que las fechas en el medio del contrato. Todo contrata tendrá algunos artículos semejantes y éstos son los unos que mencionaré como ellos pertenecen a 1-4 contratos de bienes raíces de reventa de familia en Tejas. Escogí Tejas porque soy un Corredor en Tejas y yo operan abajo leyes de Tejas.

Para comentar en contratos de bienes raíces en otros estados estaría fuera de lugar. Si usted no compra en Tejas, sin embargo, algunos de estos artículos aparecerán en algún lugar en un contrato no importa dónde se escribe. Todo trato de hacer aquí lo deberá educar acerca de seguir la compra de su sueño en casa, ganando un Ph. D. en la ley de bienes raíces no es nuestra meta.

El Precio de venta

Esto es el precio que usted concuerda en pagar el vendedor para la casa. Este precio puede cambiar durante el curso de la transacción. Una razón común para el precio de venta para cambiar es porque el valor de mercado valorado de la casa es más bajo que el precio de venta.

El Desembolso Inicial

Esto es la cantidad su oficial del préstamo ha dicho usted será requerido a obtener su préstamo. Estas cantidades se fijan generalmente en 3%, 5%, 10% o 20% del precio de venta total. Usted puede poner hacia abajo más que el mínimo requirió, pero se cerciora a su oficial del préstamo es informado de este plan. **No obtenga esta cantidad confusa con costos finales.**

Sus costos estimados del fin incluirán el desembolso inicial pero consisten en muchos otros costos. Los honorarios de costumbre que son una parte de costos finales son los honorarios relacionados a obtener su préstamo, los impuestos prepagados, el interés y el seguro, los honorarios relacionados a su política del título, a los honorarios de mensajero y mensajero, y a los honorarios de abogado para denominar apenas unos pocos. **Su desembolso inicial más estos honorarios compone sus costos del fin del TOTALES.** Por eso cuando "no Dinero hacia abajo" es indicado en un anuncio, nunca significa que usted no tendrá dinero que sale de su bolsillo. Puede significar simplemente que 100% de financiamiento se puede obtener bajo las circunstancias anunciadas, pero bajo no significa que eso no habrá cualquier otros costos finales implicados.

La cantidad financió

Esto es la diferencia entre el precio de venta y el desembolso inicial. Es la cantidad que el banco financiará verdaderamente. Hay a veces las primas añadieron a este que será calculado luego tal como la prima de seguros de la hipoteca de FHA (si usted obtiene un préstamo de FHA).

Financiar la Fuente

Hay el apéndice diferente (formas añadieron al contrato que dirigen detalles específicos de la venta) para tipos diferentes de la financiación. Su profesional de bienes raíces sabrá cuál utilizar basado en su financiamiento. Esto es otra gran razón para de la aprobación pre. Si durante el curso de la transacción su oficial del préstamo decide que ese financiamiento de FHA sería mejor para usted que un préstamo convencional que el contrato debe ser reordena acomodar los cambios. Note que un cambio en el financiamiento puede afectar al vendedor es los costos finales y si el vendedor nega el cambio en el financiamiento usted puede encontrar que usted es fuera de contrato.

Titule la Compañía (Oficial del fideicomiso)

La Compañía del Título es el poseedor del "dinero serio" si su contrato se escribe con dinero serio. En Tejas, dinero serio no se requiere a agregar la validez a su contrato, sin embargo, el vendedor no le puede dar el tiempo de día sin lo. Se puede ver como su interés serio en Comprar la propiedad. La Compañía del Título también manejará normalmente la búsqueda del título y cerrará la venta. Un abogado puede actuar como también en oficial del fideicomiso y cerrar su venta.

El Comprador puede escoger la Compañía del Título o en caución oficial, sin embargo no es untypical para el Vendedor de escoger. Usted encontrará esto ser un artículo negociable en el contrato. Generalmente, si el vendedor será particular acerca de esto, ellos lo indicarán arriba frente. También, la nota que la agencia que tiene el en caución no tiene que ser la misma compañía que proporciona la política del título.

La examen

Su prestamista ordenará normalmente una examen de la propiedad. Este documento es importante porque lo dice donde las fronteras legales de su propiedad empiezan y terminan. También le dice los límites de servidumbres y si hay tuberías subterráneas que usted debe estar enterado de. Una vez que la inspección está disponible, usted tiene el derecho de pedir que el prestamista para verlo y sea

satisfecho consigo antes de fin. El tiempo de manejar la tubería que corre por el centro de la propiedad es definitivamente antes de cerrar. Muchos propietarios no verifican la inspección hasta que algo falle. Cuándo algo falla saldrá de alguien embolsa.

La Revelación del vendedor

Esto es un documento que el vendedor ha completado que detalla los artículos que el vendedor es informado acerca de que son conectados a la propiedad, eso viene con la propiedad, eso sucedió a la propiedad o eso se ha reparado o ha sido tratado en la propiedad. *No dependa de este documento para privarse una inspección*.

La Condición de la propiedad

Los detalles de la condición de la propiedad que es aceptable a usted es probablemente el la mayoría del confundiendo, la sección necesaria y entendida mal del contrato. El comprador indica aquí que ellos "acepta la propiedad en su condición presente, proporcionó al Vendedor en el gasto de Vendedores, completará el siguiente las reparaciones y los tratamientos específicos", entonces hay un espacio proporcionado para usted llenar lo que usted quiere. Lo que pasa con esta sección es que en muchos casos, el Comprador no sabe lo que, si nada necesita la reparación, porque la

---

Citado de la Comisión de bienes raíces de Tejas promulgó 1 - 4 forma de la familia, el artículo 7(d).

necesidad para reparaciones no puede ser obvia. A veces las reparaciones pueden ser obvias. Si usted compra una casa que se poseyó previamente, es posible que haya las reparaciones necesarias incluso si se notara que el dueño tomó el cuidado excepcional de la casa.

Mi sugerencia, especialmente en el caso de un previamente poseído deberá enfocar en casa en las cosas que rendirían la casa inhabitable, peligroso e insanitario. El reemplazo de una bombilla indicó en un contrato hace muy probable irrita aún vendedor más concienzudo y avergüenza gravemente a su agente que tiene que presentar esta cosa (su oferta). No es un cuento enteramente diferente si los alambres eléctricos que llevan a la instalación fija ligera se fríen o allí. ¿Entiende usted? Otra vez esto es un área susceptible, pero es práctico es la llave.

El Servicio residencial Contrata

Los contratos residenciales del servicio, se refirieron a veces a como en casa las Garantías pueden ser un artículo importante de tener. Estos contratos proporcionan alguna certeza que artículos tales como instalación de cañerías, eléctrico, el aire condicionado, las piscinas, los comejenes, y los aparatos (no una toda lista inclusiva como cada garantía es diferente), que se incluyó con su compra puede ser reparado o puede ser reemplazado si necesario para un honorario nominal. Su contrato indica que el Comprador puede comprar tal contrato y el Vendedor reembolsará al Comprador en cerrando a una cantidad que el Comprador especifica. Si usted quiere uno, esté seguro que esta sección no se deja blanco. Revise las garantías diferentes para encontrar que uno convino mejor a sus necesidades.

La Fecha final & la Posesión

Esto es un tema muy importante. En este día de adelantamiento tecnológico, closings puede suceder tan temprano como 5-10 días después que el contrato se ha firmado y ha sido colocado en en caución. Usted no necesita apresurarse este proceso. Habrá los factores en su vida que puede afectar esta fecha tal como la conclusión de su término actual de arrendamiento o la venta de su casa actual. Una agenda típica para un fin es 30-45 días. La posesión de la propiedad ocurre típicamente en la fecha que la venta ha cerrado y ha financiado (todo dinero ha cambiado de mano). A veces el comprador necesita mover en más temprano o a veces el vendedor necesita más tiempo de mover. En cualquiera de estos casos que usted necesita poner en escritura lo que usted significa. Yo nunca pienso es una idea buena para el comprador de mover en temprano ni para el vendedor para permanecer más tarde, pero estas situaciones ocurren. Mi consejo lo deberá cerciorarse especifica las condiciones de cualquiera tales ocurrencias y los trata como una transacción legal o usted pueden estar en para unas pocas sorpresas no deseadas.

Las Provisiones especiales

Esto contendrá sólo los hechos acerca de la venta que no puede ser manejada por otro apéndice.

Las notas

Esta sección del contrato detalla la información de comprador y la información de vendedor. Esta información se utiliza para mandar la correspondencia importante al comprador y el vendedor durante la transacción.

El arreglo y Otros Gastos

Esta sección es traída a su atención porque lo proporciona una lista del fin normal cuesta a un Comprador o un Vendedor pagaría. Los gastos adicionales que el Vendedor se ha pedido se pagar hacia gastos de Comprador debe ser escrito en para el Vendedor para ser responsable de esa cantidad.

El acuerdo de Partidos

Esta sección lista todos los apéndices que son una parte del contrato. Un apéndice es un documento que se ha hecho una parte del contrato y tiene detalles de negocio que pertenecerán a la venta. Por ejemplo un No Apéndice de Bienes raíces se puede hacer una parte del contrato si tanto el comprador como el vendedor concuerdan que una arandela y el secador se harán una parte de la venta. Un apéndice será añadido al contrato como creído necesario por su profesional de bienes raíces. Si el título del apéndice no está en la lista impresa, entonces su agente lo debe agregar a la "Otra" sección. Un apéndice que forma parte de su contrato se debe listar como tal o técnicamente, no existe como parte del contrato.

La Opción de la terminación

Un Comprador puede comprar un derecho sin restricción para terminar el contrato con un honorario de la opción. Sin restricción simplemente medios incluso si su perro lo muera puede terminar el contrato, pero la nota que usted perderá su honorario de la opción. Su dinero serio, sin embargo, se reintegrará. Si usted no termina el contrato dentro del tiempo especificado, usted es obligado a los términos del contrato. El honorario de la opción puede ser acreditado al Precio de venta en el fin si el comprador continúa con la venta. Sí, usted puede hacer las inspecciones durante su período de la opción, pero sus hallazgos no obligan al vendedor a hacer cualquiera repara a la propiedad por su inspección. Las reparaciones solicitaron durante un período de la opción que no eran la parte de la llamada original del acuerdo para la renegociar del contrato si usted desea continuar con la compra.

No ASUMA QUE EL VENDEDOR CUIDARA DE CUALQUIERA REPARA UNA VEZ USTED PUEDE DEMOSTRAR QUE LA CASA CAE AL SUELO.

Consulte a un Abogado

Si el Comprador o el Vendedor han retenido a un abogado para ayudar con la venta, la información de abogado se proporcionaría en esta sección.

La Fecha de vigencia & Firmas

La fecha de vigencia del contacto es la fecha que ambos partidos (Comprador y Vendedor) se concordó. Esta fecha no es necesariamente la fecha que el documento físico se firma. Tan pronto como el vendedor acepta la oferta y notifica al Comprador de tal Aceptación, el contrato es efectivo. Esta fecha puede ser llenada por cualquier agente y manejará todos los otros detalles que deben ocurrir dentro de días especificados a través del contrato. El contrato debe ser firmado por ambos partidos para ser un documento obligatorio. (Cerciórese a su profesional de bienes raíces entrega una copia de este documento a usted.)

El Recibo de vendedores

El Vendedor completará esta sección si hay un Honorario de la Opción implicado. Si el Honorario de la Opción no se cambia apropiadamente, (El contrato indica "Comprador ha pagado a Vendedor (amount)(option el honorario) para el derecho sin restricción para terminar el contrato por avisar de la terminación al Vendedor dentro de (# días) después que la fecha de vigencia de este contrato. "), la validez del período de la opción se puede afectar.

La Información de la correduría

Esta sección detalla la cantidad de la comisión que será pagada al Corredor del Comprador por el Corredor de Vendedor. Contiene también la información del negocio para la Venta y Listar a a Agentes en la transacción. Hay los acuerdos separados que determina lo que se escribirá aquí. Ellos son el acuerdo de la Representación de Comprador entre el Comprador y el agente de comprador y el Acuerdo de la Lista entre el Vendedor y el agente de vendedor.

En caución Recibo

La Compañía del Título completará esta sección para registrar la fecha ellos recibieron dinero serio (si cualquiera) del comprador. Su dinero serio se debe volver el en caución oficial dentro de 2 días de la fecha de vigencia de su contrato.

No hay la pregunta que es estúpido cuando viene al contrato. Si hay algo dentro del contrato que usted no entiende, usted tiene el derecho de obtener una respuesta satisfactoria de su agente.

LEA SU CONTRATO. ¡SI USTED TIENE TODAVIA las PREGUNTAS DESPUES QUE LEER SU CONTRATO Y ESTA MATERIA, PREGUNTAN!

Por supuesto yo no podría detallar cada palabra del contrato, pero he tratado de proporcionarlo con algunos de los puntos culminantes. Así como cada propiedad es diferente tan hace cada contrato es diferente para cada venta. No existe un trato de cortador de galleta.

ENROLLARLO ARRIBA O HACIA ABAJO

¡Yippee!! He obtenido un contrato aceptado…He obtenido yo un contrato aceptado (usted puede oír la música?). **¿AHORA QUE?**

Bien, si usted compra una casa en "como es" la condición con el DINERO EFECTIVO, entonces fin es próximo. ¡Si no, (quizás la mayoría de casos) habrá las Inspecciones, las Evaluaciones, y las Inspecciones (Ah mi)! No olvidémosnos acerca de satisfacer sus condiciones del préstamo. Nadie en tierra lo puede preparar para este proceso, pero para yo ciertamente trataré.

La PACIENCIA se REQUIERE DEFINITIVAMENTE. Las INSTRUCCIONES SIGUIENTES no DUELEN CUALQUIERA.

Ante todo, hay personas que necesitan de obtener este contrato. Usted necesita una copia, su prestamista necesita una copia, el en caución agente (o la compañía del título), el vendedor y los agentes implicados. El prestamista empieza a completar su préstamo, la compañía del título empieza a preparar documentos para su seguro del título, usted necesita empezar a realizar sus deberes bajo el contrato y el vendedor empiezan a realizar los deberes bajo el contrato.

Cuando usted prepara para cerrar varias cosas pasan detrás de las escenas con todos partidos a la transacción. Comunicación entre todo esos implicado llegan a ser una necesidad. Aquí están algunas cosas comunes que ocurren antes usted cerrará su venta.

USTED COMPLETARA SUS INSPECCIONES. No se recomienda que esta parte se sea saltada. Si usted escoge saltarse las inspecciones, no son sorprendió si su agente pide que usted firme una renuncia. La inspección de la estructura, de los sistemas mecánicos, y del motivo para la madera insectos destructores deben ser realizados por un inspector licenciado.

Usted puede escoger a un inspector de su elección de las páginas amarillas o cualquier otra fuente usted cree seguro (Ve que el capítulo a Encontrar a Su Agente como muchas de las mismas reglas aplican). Yo no recomiendo utilizando un inspector escogido por el vendedor debido a el conflicto del intrés obvio. Si usted pide que su agente recomiende a un inspector, y el agente verdaderamente lo obliga, entonces no demanda a su agente si algo falla. Usted no está bajo la obligación de utilizar a un inspector sugerido por nadie. Esto aplica a todos vendedores que son recomendados por su agente porque usted insistió en una referencia. Si usted es demasiado perezoso hacer su propio juego de piernas, entonces no se queja acerca del resultado ni las tasas.

El costo para servicios de inspección varía. Yo lo aliento a Haga de compras alrededor para el mejor precio para el mejor servicio. Compare las tasas, comparan los servicios. Escoja uno y recuerde que ellos trabajan para usted. Asista a la inspección si en todo posible. Su agente puede asistir las inspecciones con usted o para usted, sin embargo, no es protocolo para ellos pedir que el inspector que cualquiera pregunte concerniendo los comentarios de la inspección o la marca a usted acerca de la inspección.

¡BUENO! Usted escoge hacer las inspecciones (una elección muy sabia). Las personas que renuncian su derecho de hacer esto es generalmente UN) comprando una casa nuevo o bastante nuevo (todavía una elección mala no hacer una inspección), B) inspectores sí mismos y todos sistemas son va, C) barato, D) loco. Por favor no renuncie su inspección porque usted es abajo la influencia de C o D.

Después que las inspecciones son completas, usted será presentado con los informes que indican qué reparaciones o los tratamientos (si cualquiera) son necesarios. Favor de notar que el inspector mira el casa según pautas específicas y de acuerdo con códigos actuales de edificio. Si la casa se construyó en 1955, por supuesto el informe se cargará con cosas, eso según código actual, se debe reparar o debe ser mentado para fechar. Si usted solicitan un VA o el préstamo de FHA, esto puede ser un concierne. Si no, la información se proporciona para usted determinar el inhabitability, la seguridad, y las condiciones sanitarias de la casa. Si usted ha comprado una opción y realiza la inspección durante el período de la opción, la inspección lo puede ayudar a determinar si usted quiere continuar con la venta o no.

Las inspecciones no se deben realizar porque usted piensa que su prestamista parará la venta si los hallazgos no son satisfactorio. Dependiendo del tipo del préstamo que usted obtiene, el prestamista que proporciona su financiamiento no puede tener interés en lo que su informe dice. Sé que eso es un desilusionar pequeño, pero la razón usted gastó todo ese dinero lo debía cerciorarse supo lo que su entraban en.

Mientras tanto, la espalda en la compañía de la hipoteca, y en algún punto antes cerrar, su prestamista ordenará un **INFORME DE LA VALORACIÓN**. Este informe revelará algunas cosas importantes tales como A) Es el valor de la casa el precio indicado en su contrato, B) están los asuntos allí mayores que necesitan de ser dirigidos como la línea del defecto que corre por el centro de la propiedad que ha contribuido substancialmente a la 12 grieta de la pulgada en el trozo. Esta clase del material será importante a ellos antes ellos le dan el dinero.

Permitanos la dirección el asunto de la valoración primero. Si la casa "no valora" o en términos de laico si el precio que usted concordó sobre con el vendedor es más alto que la evaluación formal, entonces la casa "no valoró." Un par de cosas pueden suceder en este momento, usted puede tratar de renegociar el precio basado en la evaluación o en es posible que el contrato pueda terminar. Usted no obtendrá. La financiación hasta que el precio se haya bajado a encontrar la evaluación. Bajo algunas circunstancias puede ser frugal pagar la diferencia - por ejemplo usted quiere la casa tan malo usted está dispuesto a pagar más que vale de tenerlo. ¿No pienso yo que esto es listo, pero qué yo sé? El vendedor probablemente no querrá lo que ha sucedido, pero la elección para ellos es "Vende" o espera al próximo comprador y una evaluación nueva. La probabilidad para una evaluación nueva que sigue rápidamente salir muy diferente del primer es delgada. Yo no dije era imposible. Puede estar en el mejor interés del vendedor de renegociar en este momento, **NOSOTROS ESPERAMOS.**

Esto menta el asunto de **PRESTAMISTA las REPARACIONES REQUERIDAS.** ¿Qué es estos de todos modos? Ellos son las cosas que el Prestamista requiere a ser reparadas para completan procesamiento de su préstamo. La evaluación es generalmente el documento que hace al prestamista requiere las reparaciones antes ellos darán dinero. Estas reparaciones implican comúnmente los problemas que harán la caída de la casa en el suelo y dañarán gravemente el valor de la reventa de la propiedad en alguna fecha futura si no cuidó de ahora. Las bases agrietadas, techos y comejenes malos son apenas algunos del prestamista común las reparaciones y los tratamientos requeridos.

Quiero indicar aquí que si para alguna razón su fuente del financiamiento escoge no hacer una evaluación (y esto sucede a veces) el vendedor no puede tener un deber para reparar lo que usted piensa es un "prestamista la reparación requerida." Apenas llamamiento un asunto con la propiedad que un prestamista requirió la reparación o el tratamiento no lo hacen un prestamista requirió la reparación o el tratamiento.

EL PRESTAMISTA LO DEBE REQUERIR Y NOTIFICAR GENERALMENTE EL COMPRADOR Y a VENDEDOR (si es verdaderamente un prestamista la reparación o el tratamiento requeridos) EN la ESCRITURA.

TIEMPO FINAL

Sus informes han entrado y ellos parecen gran, eso es la Inspección, la Evaluación, y la Inspección. ¡Whew! ¡Eso era mucho trabajo! Usted está en la mesa final. Todos sonríen (optimistamente). ¡Usted tiene el dinero, la propiedad valoró, alguna reparación o los requerido solicitados son completos, usted quiere su propiedad y usted lo quiere ahora!

Bueno…¿. Qué puede fallar en el fin?

1. Nadie lo dijo obtener el SEGURO. Sí, usted necesitará el seguro para cerrar el trato. Sugiero que usted mira a obtener algún derecho después que su contrato se firma. Escoja cualquier compañía de seguros usted desea y sí, usted será cargado una prima entera de años más 2-3 meses para su cuenta de garantía bloqueada (eso es si usted es requerido a tener uno).

2. La lámpara psicodélica en la cocina no permanece. Cuando usted y el vendedor son entrados en el discurso pequeño en la mesa, usted averigua que ellos planean tomar que lámpara psicodélica realmente fabulosa. Usted lo pensó era una parte del trato. Usted no firmará los papeles porque usted quiere esa lámpara. El vendedor no firmará la causa que él toma. Optimistamente esto nunca sucederá porque su agente con cuidado escogido lo se habría cerciorado fue informado de artículos excluidos de la compra y esos artículos sería deletreado adicionalmente en la escritura en su contrato.

3. ¿Qué usted significa no puedo mover yo en hasta la semana próxima? ¿Usted recuerda ese párrafo en su contrato que habló acerca de la posesión? Usted se cerciora mejor que el vendedor está en la misma página acerca de mover su material fuera y usted moviendo suyo en. Si habrá las circunstancias especiales, no toma nadie palabra para lo. ¡Obténgalo en escritura!

4. ¡Yo no pago por esa garantía estúpida! ¡Oops! La compañía del título hizo un error y puso esta carga en su lado. Ellos hacen los errores también. ¡Apenas calmamente el estado que el vendedor dijo que él pagaría y ellos verificarán el contrato y moverán el artículo al lado del vendedor, salvando el día! A propósito, es una idea muy buena para usted o su agente de obtener la Declaración del Arreglo (se refirió a veces a como el HUD-1) por lo menos 24 horas antes de cerrar. Esto no es justo una buena idea, pero usted tiene la derecha de repasarla antes del cierre .

Nadie puede anticipar y poder parar cada situación que podría ocurrir en la mesa final del acontecimiento, pero hay un bastantes que puede ser parado con la preparación apropiada y comunicación honesta entre todos partidos. Usted ha logrado obtener las llaves, su agente es agotado…. Ahora va y goza su casa. Cuándo usted está listo para vender, llamar a su agente y preparar a experimentar el otro lado de la transacción.

SOBRE CORINNE

Corinne Luna es corredor de propiedades inmobiliarias licenciado y corredor de hipoteca en el estado de Tejas. Ella lleva a cabo un masters en la administración del negocio de la universidad del Bautista de Houston, y los solteros del grado de la ciencia en psicología de la universidad de Houston. La casan con el Jr. de Juan Luna y tienen tres niños, Tish, Amanda y Marissa y un nieto Ahlauna.